WHY I TRIED TO DIE

D1551370

A Story of Trauma, Resilience, and Restoration

LISA KESSLER-PETERS

Paperback 978-1-945169-38-0
eBook 978-1-945169-39-7

Published by
Mercy & Moxie, an imprint of
Orison Publishers Inc.
PO Box 188, Grantham, PA 17027
www.OrisonPublishers.com

Endorsements

Come walk with Lisa as she takes you on a journey from death to life. Her testimony of how she was delivered from a life of addiction and trauma will inspire you to seek a deeper relationship with God.

Why I Tried to Die will grip you from the beginning through the end. Lisa's courageous transparency throughout the pages of this book reveal the glory of God and His redemptive healing and restorative powers. It is a must-read for all who are currently going through or dealing with trauma from the past. You will not be disappointed.

—MB Busch
President, Heartbeat of Heaven Ministries

Lisa invites the reader on a journey. This journey is the story of her life, full of hopelessness, tragedy and trauma. Yet, in the midst of the most difficult and hopeless of moments, she encountered the living God who repositioned her with a hope and a future. No life is beyond the reach of a loving God, and Lisa's story is a great reminder of this truth.

—Pastor Ruth Hendrickson
Ruth Hendrickson Ministries
ruthhendrickson.org

A riveting page-turner! Lisa's story is one of how heartbreaking trauma kept her world from being safe. But God had other plans! In the most surprising of places, *He* set her free. Her trust, resiliency and transformation are a testimony of God's power that speaks profound truth.

—Mary Whitman Ortiz
Founder, Limitless Intimacy

When reading *Why I Tried to Die*, I instantly was able to connect to the author. Her ability to capture and articulate her story to the reader was simply amazing. As someone who dealt with abuse for many years, I was able to identify with what Lisa described. As an author myself, I understand first-hand how difficult it is to not only keep the reader intrigued, but also create an imagery for the reader to experience. Lisa was able to do that as well. I believe that this book will not only transform lives, but also change the minds and stereotypes that have been in place. The author is an amazing woman, and I am blessed to have her in my life.

—Veronica Dixon
Co-Pastor, Elevated Life in Christ Community Church

What comes through for me in *Why I Tried to Die* is Lisa's amazing courage and resilience. I read her words but cannot fathom how she endured persistent childhood trauma in her home, the shuttling back and forth to foster homes and a different school every year, and exposure at such an early age to drugs, alcohol, sex and sexual abuse.

On several occasions, I have had the privilege of hearing Lisa eloquently summarize her life's journey, but the book captures what a ten-minute talk cannot—the depth of the harm she experienced and her battle to overcome the pain and trauma against all odds. Speaking with her before her initial talk, I had no clue that she was so horribly mistreated by too many for so long.

Lisa is truly a remarkable woman. Her work is an inspiration to all who read it that even the most inhuman challenges can be overcome with faith and the love of life as expressed by her devotion to her children.

—Robert K. Reed
Executive Deputy Attorney General for Special Initiatives
Pennsylvania Office of Attorney General

Dedication

I dedicate this book to my Lord to be used however He sees fit. It is because of Him that I am here and able to tell my story. I also dedicate this book to my children, Chloe, Kaydee and Dekan. You have been my motivation since the day you each were born, and I am so thankful I get to be your mother.

Acknowledgments

I want to thank everyone who supports me, especially my husband, David Peters, and my mentors, Pastor Jason Seaman and Reverend Donna Humphries. Pastor Jason, Reverend Donna, without the two of you believing and pouring into me, I know I wouldn't be as far along as I am today.

A special thank you goes to my writing coach and publisher, Marsha Blessing, and her team. Thanks for making a dream come to life.

Contents

Foreword

This is a story of an incredible journey. In my work with incarcerated women and those in recovery from addictions, I have encountered women who possess a peace Christ promised, one that passes human understanding. For many, this sacred presence of peace was forged in the storms of life. This peace and joy are precious, and Lisa writes that it was not realized in human relationships, drugs and alcohol, psychiatric hospitalizations and medications, but rather in a relationship with her Savior.

A golden strand of God's mercy and grace is woven into the fabric of Lisa's life. We see it in her earliest thoughts of God as a child and in her dark prison experience. God was her lifeline, both realized and unrealized at times. When she awoke after ingesting 300 opioid pain medications, I think she realized that God was near her.

Therefore, today we can celebrate with her the freedom she has found. We can be encouraged by God's provision for Lisa and her children. When you consider the people God brought into her life and the daily provision of places to live and finances, we see again the golden strand of God's faithfulness. A mother's heart longed for her children, and they were restored to her.

Lisa is a living example of servanthood. She shares in this book Scriptures from the Book of Isaiah that reference visiting the prisoner, even ministering to those in bondage to substance abuse. She absolutely is aware of the mercy and grace she experienced and wants for others to experience the freedom she found in Christ.

—Kathryn M. Whiteley, PhD
Criminologist
Lebanon Valley College, Pennsylvania
Producer of the documentary, *Until We Have Faces*

Introduction

My entire life I have been searching, begging and bargaining in my attempts to find happiness. I was abandoned, abused and/or neglected by all who were supposed to love, protect and care for me. I kept thinking that someone, somewhere, would bring me the happiness I so dearly needed. I was neglected since I was a young child, and I never truly had happiness except for a brief period in my life from when I was 19 till about 24 years old. But even in those years my happiness was found in others' happiness, and their failures were my failures—or so I thought. I was codependent on others like my life depended on it, and at times it did. I felt I would die if I was alone. I felt that I would take my own life. Throughout my life I have attempted and contemplated death more times than I can count.

Now, though, I have a new life. I am brand-new. The old Lisa is dead. I hope my story helps you to overcome any of the same barriers and issues I have experienced throughout my life. Today I am a humble, courageous, transparent, healthy woman. This transformation process is ongoing, though, and *you must never give up*.

I never liked it when people said, "What doesn't kill us makes us stronger." For a depressed person who is already feeling low, that statement means, "Go kill yourself. There is no point; you can't be fixed; it's too much for you to handle." If that's what you believe, I'm here to tell you that I was wrong when I believed that lie. Now, this is not a pity party. Yes, I have been through some horrible things at the hands of those who were supposed to care for me: those who made me, raised me, married me or had long-term relationships with me. I was told I was loved but not shown evidence to back that up. I am no longer bitter about what happened in my past because now I know that I was looking for love and acceptance in the wrong places the whole time. I forgot to look into my own eyes to find out who I am and what my identity is.

I wrote this book with the intent to inspire and give hope to those currently struggling with trauma, shame and hopelessness. I once believed I was tortured by being alive. I didn't realize that there was a different life available to me—and to you as well—where there is no shame and where each of us has identity and purpose.

I also wrote this book to educate Christians, caretakers and professionals who have never experienced trauma about people who have. It's important to put a face and a story to trauma and the hope that can come when it seems all hope should be gone. *Resiliency!* Miracles still happen today—we just have to keep looking up!

I have known that I was supposed to write a story about my life since I was approximately 11 years old. I even started writing it multiple times over the years. However, I would get frustrated and rip up the pages. The need to write this book has been with me for a very long time.

There is a season for everything that happens underneath the sun and stars—a time to be silent and a time to speak! (See Ecclesiastes 3:1, 7.) Now is my time! Don't let yourself get lost and never found. Life is too beautiful to miss out on!

1
Bye-Bye, Mommy

The house was silent and dark. I sat on the floor, my legs pulled close into my chest. I was positioned in front of the glass French doors in the hallway. These doors had square panels of glass you could see through, but the view was blurry. The doors separated the hallway that led to the bedrooms from the main living area, which contained the living room and the front door. The door is where my eyes were locked; I don't think I even blinked. I was confident that if anyone entered the house, I would be safe in that spot. Nevertheless, the hairs on the back of my neck were sticking straight up.

I was breathing heavily, and my heart pounded. Just moments before I had raced through the house looking for the cordless phone. I had searched in the kitchen, on the counters, in my mom's room, under the couch cushions—it was nowhere! I needed that phone and I needed it now! It was the only one in the house. Where was the phone?

Then it hit me: my mother must have hidden it before she left. But where did she go? And when was she coming back? I had to stay calm. I didn't want to wake up the others. My three siblings at the time, one older brother and two younger sisters, all were sleeping in their rooms. I did not need to worry them. They did not need to know that our mother had left us all alone. At that moment, the caretaking started. I *needed* to protect everyone involved. I had to do something to change the situation in which we found ourselves.

My brother was the oldest; he was seven years old then. I followed in age and was six. Then in order came my little sisters who were only three and four. The urge to protect them was so strong. I didn't know what was going on that night, but I just knew something was not right.

I continued to sit curled up on the floor, watching and waiting. I was tired and more scared than I could ever imagine, but I felt strong at the same time. I didn't know what I was waiting for, but something bad was happening. I could feel it inside of me.

I stared so deeply at the front door that I thought I would burn a hole through it.

Finally, I heard voices and the jingling of keys outside the front door. I inched to my left so that my body was out of sight behind the wall. The house was completely dark, but I figured the light would be turned on once "they" entered.

Wait! Who were they? I figured one was my mother, but who else? My mind raced, and the more I thought about who was out there, the more scared I became. I heard laughter and deep voices.

When the door opened, my mom entered first, followed by a few dark, scary figures that weren't familiar. Once the light was switched on, I saw two, maybe three, males with motorcycle helmets, leather vests and rough appearances. I was petrified! These men were huge, especially compared with me. I was a scrawny little redhead. Just picture little orphan Annie; that was me. I often felt like Annie, too—neglected and forgotten! I felt abandoned as a child, and it was a slippery slope from a life of abandonment to trust issues from then on. I retreated into my shell of repression to handle what was happening.

My mother was laughing and talking even louder than normal. She has a voice that can carry across a crowded room. My mother and her male friends with their long hair, facial hair, bandanas and six packs of beer migrated to the room connected to the living room. It was our sitting room, which had the television in it.

I was still very scared but somewhat relieved that she was home. I couldn't watch anymore. I felt nauseated to the point that I could taste the vomit in my throat. I crawled into my room without being detected because the hallway remained dark even with the living room lights on. I lay in my pink canopy bed, crying into my pillow in order to muffle my sobs. I heard moaning coming from the living room, and I cried harder and covered my ears with my hands.

I was six years old, only six. I was just a baby! But I was no longer a child. I knew, or thought I knew, what they were doing, even though I was confused.

At one point while I was watching the adults in the living room from my spot in the hallway, I said to myself, "It's not supposed to be like this!" Then a crazy thing occurred: a voice responded and said, "You're right, and you're going to do something about it. You're going to have a safe haven for my children." The voice was not my voice, yet no one was there with me. Had I just heard the voice of God? Or did I simply have a wild imagination? That voice, though, ignited something in me that day. *Someday I would have a safe place for children.* This became a passion of mine.

The next day I stayed quiet and tried my best to be myself while still being so fearful of what would happen. I knew instinctively that our mother leaving us alone wasn't a one-time deal. I figured, since she felt she was successful at leaving us after we went to bed, she would continue to do so. I was right.

My mother came home at all hours of the night. I never slept. I was on constant alert. All the while, I wondered what was going on with my mom. Why was she drinking all of a sudden? Was it my fault? I started to self-blame, so I became the caretaker, the protector. I always felt that I had to protect others against everything, even themselves. I felt responsible for other peoples' happiness, but I was so sad and depressed. The stress these beliefs were putting on me was too intense. I felt like a ticking bomb.

Then, out of nowhere, my mom okayed for my father to take us for a day, after years of refusing to allow us to see him (except my brother, who was a handful but also without proper parenting). I was shocked, scared, nervous, excited and hopeful. I didn't remember the last time I had seen my father, and my mom spoke of him poorly, to put it nicely. He was "the devil," my mom would say. To a six-year-old, that meant he literally was the devil. I expected a red-horned creature engulfed in flames. Whoa! Why would she let us go with him if he was the devil? My brother went with him often, but we girls didn't. My dad probably took my brother as much as my mom could get him to. My mother couldn't handle my older brother. Mom was only in her early 20s with four kids, but I didn't see her age; I saw her simply as my mother, the one who was supposed to take care of her children.

My father came and picked us up. I was so nervous! He said he was taking us to the park. My anxiety slowly decreased, and before I realized what I was saying, I had told my father the whole story of what my mother was doing. It was as if it all came out in one breath, I had held it in for so long. I was getting good at repressing pain and fear. More pain? Just add another layer I would later have to deal with.

My father was infuriated, and he decided immediately that he wasn't bringing us back home to my mother!

Sitting in a dark hallway, afraid and alone, waiting for my mother, is my first clear memory. That night so long ago is also the first time I remember experiencing a cycle of depression that always sent me into a hole deeper than most people could ever imagine, especially in a young, sweet girl whose innocence was lost. I hated myself when others had problems because I couldn't save them. I thought I was going to change the world and make it a beautiful place for kids to live in....

2
The Grass Is Not Greener on the Other Side

I thought for a split second life would get better, now that we were out of my mom's care. I was extremely mistaken. My mother did not put up much of a fight for us because she wanted to be freed from the burden of having four children at a young age. That was the impression I had at the time. She had taken on too much and was at her breaking point. She was only a teenager herself when she started having children.

I knew my mom was different from other moms, but I didn't understand why. She was fighting her own mental-health battles. She was bipolar and was a binge drinker. She never would stay on her medication to help with the highs and lows; she constantly would discontinue taking her medications, stating that it was because of the side effects she would have. For example, weight gain, tendency to oversleep, lack of energy and lack of personality are some side effects that come with a lot of psychiatric mood stabilizers. I know for a fact that some side effects of medications can be unbearable; however, one must weigh the pros and cons of being on medication as well as what additional and/or alternative methods of treatment are available.

A long line of mental health problems and alcohol/drug abuse run through both sides of my family. Many have gone undiagnosed because of a lack of knowledge and the acceptance that everybody has weaknesses. As a result, we have to do self-care in order to live a productive, happy life. It's easier to be someone who doesn't have a diagnosis or an addiction than to address it. I battled this tendency for 22 years of my life. (I will talk more about this later as I describe my own struggles with identifying myself and who I had become.)

The truth is, I thought our family was unique in our chaos. I have come to find out since then that some families just hide their problems better. I think it is worse to believe you are alone in this fight than to know others battle with the same things. It can be encouraging to know that all families struggle with something, whether it is addiction, mental health or another stress. It takes away the stigma that your family is just broken and without hope.

Let me get back to my story. I was a little girl thinking of her dream life and family. I just wanted a mommy and a daddy who cared for me and were around, but that didn't happen. My father, prior to deciding to take us in, had been living in an efficiency apartment. It was a one-bedroom apartment that had a community bathroom and kitchen—not a place for a child to live or be raised. Usually single men occupied these rooms. My father had no time to make arrangements for a bigger place because it was an emergency situation. He called his sister and asked if we (my dad and us kids) could go stay there in the meantime. The "meantime" seemed like forever. Now seven children and two adults were sharing a household. Yes, I admit that at first I thought it was awesome; I could play with my cousins all the time and had two people to take care of me. False! Wrong answer! It never happened.

The problem was neither my dad nor my aunt functioned well enough to be a good role model. They both drank daily and smoked marijuana. They also did other drugs and smoked crack, but I didn't know that back then and I'm happy that I didn't. I already knew way more than a young child should at that age. I remember bits and pieces of us living with my aunt and dad. For example, they took turns stepping out of the house for days and leaving the other one to handle the chaos of the home. Sometimes they both went out and left me in charge, even though I was only seven and could barely reach the stove, even while standing on a chair. I had started cooking at six years old while living with my mom. Privacy didn't exist. Sometimes the adults would lock us out of the house without food and we would end up scavenging for food from neighbors or stealing.

My dad taught me how to be a good thief. He even used me in his schemes. I was the decoy. Whenever he went out to steal, he brought me in the store with him while the rest of the kids waited in the car. The two of us would go into department stores. The plan of action would go like this: my dad and I enter the store, he grabs a cart, and we quickly grab a big-priced item like a television, a set of tools, a vacuum—whatever was expensive but fit in the cart. Then we would go to the customer service department in the store, and he would return the item. They would give him store credit because he didn't have a receipt, and he would then use the store credit at a different location to buy cartons of cigarettes. After that he would sell the cigarettes. Sometimes he took us to New York City and made us stand on the streets selling packs of cigarettes for $1 per pack. Sometimes people thought we four kids were homeless and gave us money.

We kids didn't have rules. We all were left to learn life's lessons on our own. When it came to both child and adult stuff—from reading, riding a bike, swimming, cooking, cleaning, driving a car, doing makeup—basically everything you are supposed to be taught to do, I learned on my own. No one helped me. I cried in silent, behind closed doors, from the emotional pain I suffered. On the outside, I was a well-mannered kid who looked like she enjoyed life and had her head on straight. If only it was true! On the inside I was crying out for help the whole time, but I knew if I cried out loud, I wouldn't be heard. Rather, as I came to find out, I would be punished for being sad, depressed and suicidal. My poor heart was crying for my mom, or anyone who cared, but I knew she would never be there, especially not the way I needed her to be there.

While living with my aunt, I had this recurring nightmare that she decapitated all seven of us kids and set our heads in a row on the counter of the bathroom and was laughing. I woke up petrified every time. This dream was one of many night terrors that started to haunt me on a regular basis. Night terrors can be subconscious indicators of how damaging and unhealthy our living environment is.

Let me be clear: my aunt was never abusive to me. She was just neglectful. She lived a very unhealthy, risky lifestyle of alcohol, partying and sex. I was never taught how to be a lady. The women I was around weren't ladies at all. They were crude and loose. At first, I thought my aunt was cool because she was such a rebel (or so I thought). Later I came to learn she really was just an unemployed single mother who lived off the system and partied 24/7.

It didn't take me long to grow into codependency with all these non-functioning adults around me. They never took responsibility for any of their actions. We kids often were inside bars or hanging out at adult parties. I realized quickly that all the people who came around were only looking to party. No one took care of the kids. We were left to care for each other, and we still do today to a certain extent. Without a mother and father, it actually was good to have lots of siblings; that meant more possibilities of getting along with some of them enough to be beneficial in each other's lives. Unfortunately, we all got separated eventually.

After a good while, my father was able to get us into a four-bedroom, income-qualified apartment out of the city, in a town called Peckville. There were still issues, but they differed a bit. I had plenty of kids to play with because each house had an average of three to five kids. I hung out mostly with

WHY I TRIED TO DIE

older kids. I was crushing on older boys, which was very inappropriate at the time, but I didn't have rules other than to do what I was told. We lived cleaner. My dad drank all day, every day, but he also worked while we all went to school. It *almost* seemed like a real family.

I remember the first day we went there. It was just my dad, me and my brother. That day stands out because it wasn't often we got time with my dad for kid stuff. Usually we were told to shut up or "get outside and play!" This night, however, he acted like a real dad. We even played a board game and Chinese checkers. It didn't matter that we didn't have any furniture in the house yet; we had bonding time. It was so impactful that I still remember it today.

I was the designated mother from the time we moved there. At eight years old, I cooked and took care of my little sisters. I made sure they were bathed, dressed and had their hair and teeth brushed. I made sure they ate and did their homework. I felt like my childhood was gone at this point. I was only a kid, but I was responsible for a lot of the household duties. The control it gave me made me feel like I had a purpose and that I could control something in my very dysfunctional family.

My father was very physically abusive to my brother. My dad constantly was hitting him. I remember begging my dad to stop sometimes because I was afraid he was going to kill my brother. Fortunately for us girls, we only got hit if we did something really bad and deserved to be spanked. One time I recall being spanked was when I skipped school in first grade. My grandmother had spent the morning with us since my dad was not home. I am not sure if he was at work or what. When she left, I went back inside the house with my friend. My grandmother had forgotten her purse, and she returned to find me and my friend. I knew I was in big trouble. I got spanked by my grandmother, then the principal paddled me, and finally my father beat me with the belt. I guess I might have deserved that one! That day was another day of innocence being shattered. A pornographic video was in the VCR. My friend and I didn't know what it was when we pressed play, but it was fascinating enough that we did not turn it off.

Up to this point I had no communication with my mother. I was so angry inside for the way she neglected us. It didn't help that both of my parents had a bad habit of always talking negatively about the other one. My father was referred to as "the devil" and my mom was a "fat, crazy bitch." I knew I loved them both, but I also knew they weren't very good at being parents.

One day my father planned to go to New York City with a friend, probably to sell cigarettes on the streets. My father as well as most of his friends were into criminal activity. It should be no surprise that I picked up the same things my dad did. It was a "caught" experience for me. When something is modeled before you as a child, good or bad, sometimes you pick up that habit without even analyzing if it is good or bad. It just is.

I started stealing. I didn't think anything was wrong with it because my father, who taught me how to do it like a professional, stole. He never *told* me to steal, but as a child I watched and mimicked the things he did. For the same reason, I started smoking cigarettes and weed and drank alcohol. I watched him do it. I followed in his footsteps and stole anything and everything from the local convenience stores. I started with gum, and before I knew what I was doing, I was filling up my book bag with stuff I didn't even want or need. I had become a kleptomaniac.

Every time I got away with shoplifting, I believed I became more invisible and could steal anything I wanted. I got a high, an adrenaline rush, from it. I guess stealing was my first addiction. It was freeing to think I could get anything I wanted. Eventually I got caught. I was so embarrassed; I started crying and begged them not to call the cops. They agreed that I was okay to leave, but I had to promise to never return to the store. I turned around and started stealing from a store right down the street a few days later.

So, one day my father planned to go to New York City with a friend. My mom was to watch us kids. I was angry, but I didn't really have a say in it, so I just dealt with it like I always did. It was the first time I was with her since I left her care a few years prior. My mother took us out shopping for something, and when we returned, we discovered that somebody had broken into our house. We walked in and found my mom's boyfriend drunk and passed out on the couch. (This man became the father to three of my future siblings.) When he got up, he decided that my mother was leaving with him. When she resisted, he got angry and violent. My older brother went to the staircase and pulled the banister off the wall. He took that piece of wood and started hitting my mother's boyfriend with it. In return, the man grabbed his bottle and whipped it at my brother. By this time, they were outside, and the neighbors heard the ruckus and called the cops. The boyfriend took off down the street, while I ran and hid. I just knew what was going to happen next: the cops were coming, and we were going to be taken away.

When the police arrived, my mother told them to "just take these kids because they are no good anyway." I was not surprised my mom talked down about us like that because that's what she did best. She justified my hatred of her. There was no way she could love us and yet treat us that way. That hatred was a horrible feeling in my heart. At that point, in my mind, my mom had crossed the line one too many times. I was done with her forever. Those are the kinds of thoughts I trained myself to believe in order to survive. To me, she was dead; she had neglected us for the last time. I did not understand her mental illness and at that point I would not have cared to be told about it.

I hid under my sisters' bunk bed, but I knew the police would find me. After they rounded up us four kids, we climbed into the cop car while my mom went back to her carefree life of no children and no responsibilities.

We went to the police station and waited for a caseworker and my father to arrive. By the time my father got there, it was too late. We had already been placed in foster homes. The agency said "temporarily," but that "temporarily" turned into more than a year before my dad could prove to the court that he was a fit parent. My dad had gotten a DUI (driving under the influence) sometime around this incident with my mother's boyfriend. As a result, the agency investigated my family and found that my father needed to complete some drug and alcohol and parenting classes. My brother and I were kept together while my two little sisters were kept together in another foster home.

3
Foster Care
(No Place for a Child)

I was first placed in foster care before I was even one year old. For obvious reasons, I don't have any memories of it. However, our bodies remember trauma.

If you are unaware of the ACEs or Adverse Childhood Experiences test, I encourage you to look it up. The test typically has ten questions and asks you things about your childhood. The higher the score, the more trauma you were most likely subjected to. Out of a score of zero to ten, I scored a ten, which is the highest possible score. What that means is I am more likely to have health issues like heart disease or a chronic disease, a shorter length of life by an average of ten years, and problems like having trouble with toxic stress, sustaining healthy relationships, and difficulty keeping employment, along with other mental-health issues. It is a good thing I don't come into agreement with any of these negative issues! However, as you will see as you keep reading my story, I already have experienced most of these problems.

The foster home my brother and I were placed in had six children, including us, which was the state limit for a foster home. The foster mom had adopted the other four kids, a set of twin boys aged 12 and a boy and girl aged 10 and 14, respectively. There was no foster father; it was just the mom and her biological son, who was in his 20s and handicapped in a wheelchair. I am not sure what his medical condition was, as I was only a child, but I don't believe he had any mobility in the lower half of his body. The foster mom ran her own sub shop from the house, and us kids were her employees who got paid nothing. She woke us up at 5:30 a.m. to clean her house. She was mean and nasty. When I cried for my father, I was forced to kneel on wood in the corner until I stopped. She had a screened porch in which we were forced to stay unless we were cleaning or helping prepare food. This woman forced me

11

to eat till I got physically sick. Since I always was a picky eater and sometimes went without food, it was extremely painful to eat against my will. It wasn't because I didn't like the food; it was just more food then I could ever consume in one sitting.

My brother attempted to run away and was placed in a different foster home as a result. I eventually built up the courage to tell my caseworker how we were being treated. She removed me from the house and, I guess, investigated the other children. I never found out what happened to them, but I like to think they were saved from that horrible place.

My next foster home was wonderful even though I didn't get along with my foster sister, Ellen. She was the foster family's biological daughter and was about a year older than me. We had to share a room with bunk beds. She went to a private school while I went to public school; the two of us were like night and day. The one thing I always thought was hilarious, as I look back at that time, is that I looked more like my foster mom than her own children did. My foster mom was a redhead, and everyone always thought I was the "real" daughter. I looked more like her than I looked like my own parents. My dad has dark hair, dark eyes and dark skin. My mother has dirty-blonde hair and blue eyes. Compare that to me and my foster mom who both have fair skin, freckles and red hair. Go figure!

One time I ran away and made it all the way to my dad's house. The distance had to be at least five miles, and for someone my age and in third grade, it seemed like forever. My foster mother found me while I was running down the street, but I refused to comply and wouldn't even talk to the family. They eventually left. I continued running. When I finally got to my dad's house, it was dusk. He wasn't home. I talked to my friends who lived in the neighborhood. None of their parents would let me in their homes because they were afraid that they would get in trouble for harboring a runaway. After a while, I eventually gave up and let my friend's mom call the cops. I was so embarrassed that my attempt to be reunited with my father had been a failure, and I knew I had hurt my foster mother's heart and feelings rather badly.

I explained that I had run away because Ellen had called my birth mother an elephant and I had pulled her hair. Even though I didn't like my mother, I wasn't going to let anyone else make fun of her. I often made jokes about my mom, but that was a cover-up for the pain I was feeling for her not caring for me the way a mother should.

I had this awful night terror while I lived with this family. In the nightmare, the basement of the foster home looked like a dungeon, and my father's body parts were hanging individually from chains on the brick walls. I would have these night terrors almost every night and wake up petrified.

Being in a foster home and estranged from your family has such a traumatic impact on a child. Regardless of how devastating a child's home circumstances are, it is what that child knows. Being placed in someone else's home feels so out of place. You feel like an outsider, and you can be very confused and even angry. That doesn't even take into account if there are unhealthy things going on in the foster home. Not having protective parents and then being bounced around to many different homes caused a lot of my low self-worth and self-esteem. It was toxic stress. Children in these situations can feel like they somehow must fix the problem, and when they fail at fixing the situation, they blame themselves.

As soon as I was about to be reunited with my biological father, Ellen and I started getting along. So, for the summer after I went home and then periodically after, I visited her until my last contact to date, which has been about ten years ago.

I was so excited to be back home. When you are separated from people you love, you tend to only remember the good times. It's funny how our memories can play tricks on us if we are not careful. I guess I thought things would be different, but they weren't. Drugs, alcohol and partying were a big part of my dad's life. People were always at our place, and I often would see and hear about inappropriate sexual things. I slowly was being corrupted without even being aware of it.

4
No Faith, No Hope

My father taught us some things early on in our lives. We were raised anti-government, anti-law and anti-religion. I am not sure what we were for, but I sure do know what we were against. The government was bad. The cops were bad. Religion was bad. There were no god and no devil. Religion was for weak people who couldn't do things on their own. My dad taught me that we are born; we do whatever we have to do to survive, at any cost; we pay taxes; and then we die, go back into the ground, and turn back into dust. There was no hope in that! What damage those lessons did to us!

At the age of nine, I tried to take my life for the first time. I don't remember what the trigger was, other than I did not want a life where I felt so unloved and uncared for. I swallowed a bottle of Tylenol® and went to sleep. When I woke up, my senses did not work correctly. My vision was blurry, my hearing was out of sync—everything echoed—and when I tried to walk, I kept losing my balance. I told my dad I was sick, and, as a consequence, I was informed that I had to clean the house if I was going to stay home from school. I remember feeling even more defeated. Within a week, I tried again to take my life. This time I used a ribbon from my dress. My dress was black with white polka dots, and the ribbon was red. I sucked in my breath as hard as I could, then wrapped and tied the ribbon around my throat. I could feel my heart beating in my head. My brother walked in to tell me dinner was ready. He helped me untie and unwind the ribbon from my neck. Then my brother told my father, and rightfully so. However, instead of getting help, I got grounded. It confused me. Here I was seeking attention, needing love and care, and instead I was getting punished.

It wasn't long before my dad had to report to go to prison. I believe it involved the abuse to my brother or some assault charge. He had requested, during sentencing, to have time to find placement for us children. My sisters went to live with my mom, who by this point had given birth to four more children. I refused to go to her. By this time, I had toughened up my heart enough and forced myself to hate her. I didn't want anything to do with her. She didn't want me, so I decided I did not want her either. My brother went to my aunt. For some reason, I decided I would go stay with my neighbor and her five kids. As a result, I was still around when it was time for my dad to report to prison to start his prison sentence. He thought it would be better to head to prison by drinking a case of beer and waiting for the cops to come to get him. I was there when they came. I got the memory of watching my father be arrested and taken away to prison belligerent and resisting.

It wasn't long before I was staying at my aunt's (my mom's sister's) house with my brother. She was one of my favorite people in the whole world. She gave me some normalcy in my childhood. We attended church, went shopping, and went out to dinner. She got me interested in reading books, taking pictures, and even writing. I had the bedroom that was my grandmother's before she passed. It was a beautiful room that contained a desk with a typewriter that my aunt taught me how to type on. It was at this time that I started getting interested in writing my story; however, it was not finished yet (and, technically, still is not).

By this time, I was starting the sixth grade, middle school. I was in a new school again. This was my sixth school so far. I remember feeling less sad and more angry about how I was forced to grow up. The bouncing around was getting to me. I remember thinking at the time, *I can be whoever I want to be; these people don't even know me.* I also had raging hormones; it wasn't long before I started getting into fights. The anger had to go somewhere, and I was tired of people treating me poorly. My brother was rather aggressive toward me also. But, as I now know, he, too, had to let his anger out on someone. His acting out included him shooting me in the butt with a BB gun and ripping an earring out of my ear, taking the cartilage along with it. Eventually my brother left there and went back into foster care. Then it was just me. It is a weird thing to be one of eight children, eventually one of ten, and not live with any of them. I tried not to think about it, but when I did it felt like I was ripped apart from myself, like little pieces of me were being scattered around, and I didn't know where they landed.

I started getting into risky behavior. I had already started smoking cigarettes back when I was living with my dad. I had this great idea that if I couldn't get him to quit smoking, I would start. For some reason I couldn't understand how to inhale, so I would swallow the smoke. Now, in the sixth grade, I upgraded to smoking weed and drinking alcohol. First it was a cooler and before I knew it, I was drinking whiskey. Crazy. I threw my first party while my aunt and uncle were out for some holiday party or something, and it got out of control. Throwing a party is horrible. There were people screaming outside, having sex in the bathroom, and going through bedrooms. All I felt like I was doing was babysitting. It ended badly, with a lot of parents coming to get their intoxicated teens. Let's just say that most people weren't allowed to hang out with me after that. Me? I was just doing what I thought would make me popular. After all, I had been raised in the party scene. It was what I knew.

Eventually I hit another low point. The reality of my family structure and my loneliness got the best of me, and I tried suicide for the third time. I was 11 years old, maybe 12. My uncle had back problems and had two bottles of painkillers, which were opiates. I took as many as I could stand with milk, maybe 30 of them. I remember getting very wobbly and couldn't pick my head up very well after ingesting them. It was like my head weighed 100 pounds. I remember I wrote cards and made phone calls to a few of my friends, saying goodbye and mumbling my words. I remember being in and out of consciousness for days. While I was out, I hallucinated that there were insects and worms climbing all over me. I remember missing a week of school. I remember around the third day being propped up in a chair with pillows on the sides of me and chicken noodle soup in front of me. I never received medical care. Maybe it was because my aunt and uncle were afraid that they would be liable; I am not sure. Once I was better, it was never talked about. It was treated like I had the flu, from which I would just get better and go on with my life. The truth is, those memories *didn't* go away, and every time something was ignored, I felt a little less important.

I still don't understand why we don't talk about stuff that happened. Let me tell you, acting like it didn't happen doesn't make it go away. It *did* happen, and until it is talked about, it won't heal and get better. So much of the pain I carried into adulthood was because stuff was ignored, and I was forced to suppress a lot of very painful things. I am always talking to my kids. I refuse to have them grow up thinking they can't talk about the things that make them sad, angry and so on.

My uncle was a little weird; he would want to hang out with me and my friends. He started having issues with drinking and drugs himself. I remember he found my journal, made a copy of it, and sent it to my dad in prison. At one point he threatened me and my aunt with a gun. I ran away the next day and snuck into my friend's house, which was right up the street.

17

My other aunt on my dad's side came and got me. I became her babysitter so she could go out at night with her boyfriend. Not long after that I went to stay with my best friend and run the streets all night with no supervision. I was acting grown, but I was just a little girl. I was only 13 years old and hanging with grown men, partying, vandalizing properties and hitchhiking, thinking it was all a game.

5
Dragged Away

My father got out of prison and decided it was time for me to go live with him before "I got myself into some trouble." If he only knew what would happen. Trust me; if you are not in a healthy place and taking care of yourself, then you cannot think you can care for other people. It is not selfish to get the help you need. *It is necessary.*

I cried the whole drive from Scranton, Pennsylvania, to Carlisle, Pennsylvania. I was moving only two hours away, but it felt like I was leaving the country. Other than meeting some of the foster kids who lived with my dad's bosses, I knew no one. Me and some of the foster kids spent a summer together in the Poconos the year before. I remember breaking my collarbone and my father having to drive me to the hospital drunk on the Fourth of July. My dad's bosses owned a campground in the Poconos and decided to relocate to a campground in Carlisle. So we moved. This was the 14th time I had moved in 13 years of life. I was so over it.

To add to it all, my dad and I lived in a motel room together. Yes, we shared a room. It was awful. If he came home from the bar with a lady, I was in the bed right next to his. Yes, that will leave a permanent scar. It wasn't long before I went to barns and started huffing gasoline. Yes, you read that right. I was inhaling gasoline. Do you know what happens when you do that? You instantly start to hallucinate. I would be facedown on the rocks, hallucinating that the rocks were a fence and there were screaming children on the other side of the fence that I could not get to, to rescue. Every time I huffed that gas, I was killing brain cells at a rapid rate, but at least I couldn't feel any pain for those couple of minutes. We finally moved into a trailer on the same property. This trailer was meant for camping, not living in, but it was better than the motel room. At least I had a room, even if it didn't have a door, just a sheet I hung up for privacy. None of my siblings were with us; it was just me and my dad.

My friends thought my dad was so cool because he let us drink and smoke marijuana. I thought it was horrible. I just wanted a parent. Only two friends at the time knew the abuse I started to endure. They often came and picked me up after I was abused, and I stayed with them for days or weeks until my dad made me come home. My one friend came to my house more than once to help rescue me in the middle of a suicide attempt. I was used to the verbal and emotional abuse; that I had endured my whole life from both parents. But I was not prepared for the physical abuse that started. I became a punching bag for my father. I believe he subconsciously looked at me like I was the wife. I had to make sure dinner was ready when he got home from work. I had to work on the weekends at an under-the-table job as a house-keeper at a hotel nearby. My dad wanted me to give him the money I earned, but he also wanted me to buy my own hygiene products and help buy the food. A lot of times, I ate food from a can.

I ran away a few times. Once two of the foster kids who lived on the same property and I robbed the safe in the store of the campground and hitchhiked to Scranton. We made out with over $300 each and blew it all. We ended up splitting up, and I was on the run for weeks before someone's parent called the cops on me.

That was the first time I went into a prison cell. Being raised with no re-spect for authority, I talked back when picked up. The cops told me they were supposed to search my things, but they wouldn't unless I gave them reason. I proceeded to say something like, "I don't know, maybe I will shoot you in your head, pig!" Needless to say, I was handcuffed, searched and placed into a holding cell until my dad arrived hours later to get me.

Now I had hit puberty. My dad's friends made comments about me "fill-ing out nicely," and my dad agreed. That still makes me sick to my stomach, thinking about that. I was in eighth grade—the grade my daughter is in as of this writing. I can't imagine someone saying that about her. I would knock that person out. But there was no one there to protect me. I was a kid living in hell on earth. Sometimes I tried to call for help, but my dad simply pulled the phone cord out of the wall. There were no cellphones then. Neighbors and friends would see my dad dragging me by my hair and look the other way. It was like no one ever noticed there was a child being neglected or abused.

On one of the worst days of my life, my father molested me. My father. The man who was supposed to protect me. The man who had me swear to wait until I was married—who even had me write on piece of paper that I swore to wait until marriage when I was around nine years old and made me put that paper in a Bible—and threatened me with chastity belts, took away the most fragile thing about me. (It still confuses me why we even had a Bible and why he used it since he was an atheist. Maybe it was because courtrooms use Bibles to swear on.)

I dissociated to survive the assault. I went away inside of myself to protect myself from what was happening. I blamed myself as well. Why did I drink that beer with him? Why did I have shorts and a tank top on? Why did I say yes when he offered to rub my shoulders because my injury from my collarbone was hurting? Why couldn't I be a grown-up and get away from here? As soon as it was over, he ran out the front door and did not come back for days. I was left alone in the house after going through that, and I said nothing to no one.

It was also around this time that I was introduced to crack cocaine. My father and his friend came home from the bar late one night. I was in bed sleeping. I remember it was a school night. They woke me up and asked me to come smoke with them. When I refused, they told me it wasn't an option and pinned me in between the couch and the table until I smoked it. I remember staying up all night and even going outside and playing in mud in the rain. After that night, I developed insomnia and hardly ever slept.

This same friend of my father had me in his vehicle one day and tried to talk to me about sex. He was wanting to find out if I was sexually active. He was very suggestive. Finally, I took off out of the car, got on my bike, and didn't return until late in the night. I remember just riding around town, trying to figure out what I was going to do.

Around the same time, my father's other friend had his grandson come in from Philadelphia. Then my dad and his friend took off for the day and left the two of us alone. I never knew this kid before that day. He tried to force me to have sex with him. When I put up a fight, he stated, "Well, I'm getting something from you, so give me head." I gave in. I never saw that kid again after that day. I never told anyone about that, either. What was the point, I thought. No one was going to protect me anyway. I started to think that sex was the only value I had that people saw in me.

I also developed an eating disorder at this age, which lasted for two decades. My father made a comment that I should make sure I "don't get fat like your mother," and something about that comment hit me in my core. It was a joke, in a crude way, but it was not to me. I got fearful and started thinking that I would get fat, or that I was already overweight and could not tell. That comment caused such a reaction in me, that fat was something I *had* to control, that I developed physical dysmorphia. For those who don't know what that is, physical dysmorphia is a compulsive obsession with one's physical appearance, in which the person often sees things about themselves that others do not. I developed anorexia and starved myself. Then I developed bulimia, throwing up after eating. I cycled between the two. Till this day I don't own a scale in my home because of it. I am comfortable in my skin today, but I am mindful of where I come from with this issue. For me, this disorder was more about having control and less about the food.

As you can imagine, I psychologically was unable to handle all that was going on and thought about killing myself quite often. I started using acid and other drugs, lacing weed with angel dust (PCP or phencyclidine) and cocaine. I became sexually promiscuous and had no value for my body or my life. I started cutting myself at this time as well. I used razors, mostly. Once I punched my mirror out of frustration and used a shard of glass to cut away at my arms and legs. I had to wrap my arm in a stretch bandage to go to school because it was that bad. I was only 14 years old and in the ninth grade. My gym teacher did not buy the story I made up about me injuring my arm; she wanted me to unwrap the bandage. When I finally did, she saw the dozen or more deep lacerations to my forearm. Crisis intervention was called, and I was admitted to the psychiatric facility at a local hospital for the first time.

I think I was relieved. For once, I felt safe. I slept like a baby. I was the only child on the unit and got so much attention. I loved it. I did so well. People cared and would listen to what I had to say. By the fifth day, they said I was getting discharged. I freaked out. I could not go back. I told them enough information that I wouldn't have to go home, but not so much that my dad would get arrested. I loved my dad. I didn't want him to get in trouble—I just didn't want him to hurt me anymore. I needed to be safe. My friend's family agreed to become kinship care (foster parents) just so I could stay with them. But my father fought against it. During family court, my father stated, "If she doesn't want to live with me, then she can go and live with strangers."

So, I ended up in a foster home, newly released from the psychiatric hospital. I was on psychiatric medication and was still quite messed up. The family I moved in with was amazing. They were loving, kind and compassionate. I didn't know what to do with that. I acted out to try to push them away. I still contemplated suicide often. My foster mother, though, was so understanding. She was adopted at birth and had such a heart for people. She was truly a follower of Jesus. I remember all the stories she shared about the children she took care of. She did the Fresh Air program for inner-city kids and had 17 foster kids total over her time of fostering, including me. She also wrote to people in prison. I remember she had a post office box just for this purpose. The thing I remember about her the most is that she really did love people. You could tell that not by what she said, but by how she acted. She put love into action. Part of that was giving me rules. It was hard to follow rules when I had been raising myself for as long as I could remember. Now all of a sudden, I wasn't allowed to be left alone at home at the age of 15. It was frustrating for me. I felt like I was being treated like a baby, but in reality, my foster mother was trying to protect me from myself.

Thank goodness I got to stay at the same school and didn't have to move the rest of my high school years. Even though I loved to run wild, get into fights, party and engage in risky behavior, I tended to be a nerd during school hours. I was in college prep and honors classes, so most of my friends in school and outside of school were different. I started dating a senior and really thought I was special. I had no self-worth, no identity and no respect for myself. I thought it was better to be seen as hard, tough and popular than it was to hold myself to any morals and values. This is the mind-set of many girls who are sexually abused early on in life or who don't have a healthy relationship with a father figure. We seek attention, any attention. Now that I was getting some, I thought things were starting to seem regular…whatever that means.

6
A Defining Moment

One day on the school bus someone said she met my two little sisters. I responded that that was impossible because they lived two hours away from me. The girl said, "No, I met them today, and they told me their names. They said they moved in with your dad." I completely lost my entire mind in that second. I don't know what I was saying, but, on the inside, I was screaming: *That can't be possible! They are not safe! I have to save them!*

I spilled out everything that had happened to my foster mother as soon as I got home. I remember more about what I felt than what I said. I do have some of it written down in a journal, though, and that helps with these memories. I told because it was no longer about me. I had never told anyone what my dad did because I knew telling would not have undone it. I had two friends with whom I disclosed the abuse back around the time it happened, but I swore them to secrecy. Nothing could undo the things he did to me. However, now I had to speak up. I had to protect my sisters from it happening to them. I remember the detectives coming to the house. I was so intimidated by them. I asked that they leave their guns in the car because they made me nervous. The detectives were a black female and a white male. They asked me a million questions. Some of the answers I couldn't give because I had dissociated myself from what was happening to me at that moment. As these two detectives talked to me, I imagined them going and arresting my dad. That made me sad. I never wanted my dad to go to jail; I just didn't want him to hurt anyone else. I wanted him to get help, to get sober. It was so painful.

The time leading up to the trial was devastating for me. My entire family disowned me. My siblings were told I had made up the abuse because I was jealous that they got to live with my dad. My family made up lies that I had put myself in foster care and declared I had lied about my dad abusing me because I wanted to date a black boy, which was something my father never would have let happen. He had some very distasteful words to say about interracial relationships and wasn't afraid to share his opinion. I think his racial attitude actually made me more curious than anything else, and I often befriended people outside my race just to see what the big deal was. To this day, some of my favorite people in the world are not white, and I think that is great.

A few times I wanted to just retreat from the whole thing because of how much my family was hating on me. One day my mom called me and asked if it was a lie. I couldn't believe that I was finally telling the truth of what happened to me and no one believed me. Of course, my foster mom believed me. She stood by me the whole time.

Let me tell you, being the victim in a trial is hard. You get asked the same question 20 different ways with the purpose of trying to trip you up. (Going on the stand and talking about what my father did to me is something I cannot forget, but for a long time I tried to.) At the same time, your family is on the stand against you trying to discredit your character when they don't even have a relationship with you. It is horrendous! I wanted to die the entire time.

The court proceedings started in August of 1998 and carried on until January 29, 1999. On December 29, 1998, I wrote:

To hear the lies is what hurts the most.
To feel as if it is my fault
when they are the ones to blame.
It is a pattern of broken promises that keeps repeating that
makes me feel this way.
As if I was wrong.
They are weak.
They can't even stand up and speak;
they just avoid the whole matter and run like cowards—
they run far away.
I feel rejected like I have my entire life,
and I am sick of being the one to cry and hurt.
I feel so alone. I have no family that loves me.
I don't have anyone to hug me when I can't stop crying.
I have no one to hold my hand when I feel like I'm dying.
I am afraid I will be like this forever and be alone forever—
alone and afraid.

I wrote this second poem on the same day:

It's so cold and bitter.
Can't you hear me screaming?
I cry out to you, but no response.
I pray for you and wish you only good, but you avoid me.
Traffic is jammed and I sit here and wait for what???
That is the question!
I put my all into everything I truly want because they say
that is how things get done, but it's all about luck.
No matter how hard I try nothing will occur unless I have
luck and even then, after a while, the luck disappears.
It's like when you first learn to ride a bike.
Your parents buy you the prettiest bike.
So you take the bike out and learn to ride it.
You love your bike, and you ride it as much as you can.
And then one day you wake up and it's gone.
You finally save enough and try your best to get a new one;
then you fall in love with that bike and again it disappears.
The chain of events keeps occurring and no matter how hard
you try, they keep disappearing.
Finally, you give up and you just walk everywhere alone
without your bike.

I share these poems I wrote at that time so you can hear the disparity I felt at that moment in my life. This was where my mind was most days.

My father was sentenced in March of 1999. The jury came back "guilty" on a few different charges and hung (which happens when a jury cannot agree upon a verdict) on the heavier charges. I was not willing to go through another trial. As I look back, it was weird that the same week the trial took place, I had Winter Gala at school. I tried to go about being a teenager, but I always felt so much like an outsider. I hated that I had this bizarre life when all I really wanted was a cute boyfriend and good grades in school.

Such a huge void existed in my life. I thought that if I only had someone to love me, that void would be fixed. I would get so invested in my relationships that I would settle and compromise myself. I really had no value for myself and so got into situations that I didn't know how to get out of. Often, I took a longer time to get over a breakup than the time we were together.

7

I'm Grown Now

I started dating my foster brother's best friend, Alan, at the age of 17. I threw all of myself into this relationship. The night before I turned 18, I got into a fight with my foster mother and thought it would be a great plan for me to move out the next day. I was fighting for freedom over my life and felt that my foster mother was holding me back. We had gotten into an argument over my going to a store to buy a birthday outfit after work without her permission. This department store shared the same parking lot as the restaurant I was working at, and I thought her restriction was ridiculous. To go from parenting yourself your whole life to having someone try to parent you is a difficult thing to do, let alone when that foster parent is strict in some ways. So, I decided I was moving out. And I did, first thing the next morning.

I moved in with Alan and his mother and a few months later we moved into our first apartment. It was great at first, but then I couldn't figure out why I wasn't feeling whole, healed and satisfied. I was still in high school—my senior year—and I was working full time at a call center for Williams Sonoma˚. The 15-hour days plus homework started to get the best of me. I loved school. I loved learning. But I had to make money to pay for my place. One thing I didn't realize about Alan is that he loved his car more than me—or anything else, for that matter. He was an entitled teen, which was something I really couldn't fathom. I had no paradigm for that. So, every paycheck he got was already spent on all the upgrades he was doing to his car or on going places with his car club. On top of that, he had problems keeping a job, so a lot of the financial weight fell on me.

Eventually, I had to go to my principal and tell her about the weight I was carrying by working full time and going to school full time. She apologized that there was nothing she could do for me since the school year had already started. I told her that I would have to drop out if she couldn't help me. She just apologized again. I was devastated. School was my outlet; I couldn't have that taken from me! Frustrated, I dropped out of high school halfway through the year. I felt like a failure.

I went to the local community college and took my GED test the same week I dropped out. I scored so high on my test that I got a diploma in the mail. I started taking college courses for criminal justice that spring semester. I ended up starting college before I would have even graduated with my high school class.

Life was still hard. My father had been corresponding with me through the mail. I wrote to him that I forgave him, but I really wanted him to acknowledge what he had done to me. He partially took responsibility, but in the next letter he recanted and justified himself. That caused me some more heartache. At the same time, I felt I was being ignored by my boyfriend. Out of rage over the two incidents happening at the same time, I took a kitchen knife and stabbed it though my forearm. Obviously, that didn't do anything to help, and by the end of the night I had locked myself in my room and downed a bottle of pills. Alan called an ambulance, and the next thing I know I'm having charcoal forced down my throat through a tube and I'm fighting against the desire to fall asleep. I was combative and angry that they even tried to save me. I was tired. I didn't want to keep living this way. (Little did I know that it wasn't the worst of it yet.) I was in the psychiatric ward for five days and then released.

It always felt so weird being released. It's like there is a sign on your forehead saying, "Watch out, I'm crazy!" I was always trying to convince the psychiatrists that I was indeed crazy, and they always replied, "No, you're not, you just have a lot of sadness," and tried some different combination of pills. Oh, how I hated the pills. They all had side effects. Some of the side effects made me feel worse than how I felt without them. Some of the side effects made me feel crazier than I already felt.

8
College

I loved school. Now in college, I really fell in love with learning. I loved to take notes. I loved to study. I loved that I got to control this part of my life. I excelled at it; it was amazing. Eventually I got some sense and broke up with Alan. I started dating one of my best friends from high school; his major was the same as mine, criminal justice. School was great. I had a new boyfriend. My job was awesome; I had landed a job as a hostess at a restaurant and two weeks later became the banquet manager. I was only 19, and I felt like I was living the dream.

However, I still had a lot of destructive feelings about my life and where I came from. I had no support system. I partied like a normal college student (well, actually a little extra). I normally had the parties at my house: beer pong, kegs in the bathtub, weed, cocaine—the whole nine yards. I thought it was all normal kid stuff, never realizing how much I put myself at risk.

I was living the dream. For the first time, I felt like a normal person doing normal things. I thought the past was behind me. I was free. I survived.

Unfortunately, that relationship didn't last because both of us were a little too free and both of us made some childish mistakes. One day, jealous and emotionally hurt, I decided to jump out of my boyfriend's vehicle while he was driving because he wouldn't stop the car. I ended up with an entire layer of skin coming off. I was scraped up from head to toe. He dropped me off at his mother's house and went back to the party. I had some significant injuries, and his mother warned me that day, as she bathed me and took pebbles out of my skin, that alcoholism ran in their family. I decided to leave him on the spot, but I was very sad about it. I really did love him and had believed we would do great things in the criminal justice field someday. (Fun fact: we both work in criminal justice today and have completely forgiven one another.)

I got a new job as a receptionist at a manufacturing and distribution business across the street from the local community college. It was a perfect setup. I could work all day, get off at 4:30 p.m., and make it to class by 5:00 p.m. every day. One day I felt like I was having a heart attack and was so scared that I ended up under my desk. I called a friend, and she took me to her family doctor. He told me I had a panic attack and prescribed Ativan*, 0.5 mg, for me. I was never informed that it was addictive. I didn't even find out that it was a benzodiazepine and realize the long-term effects that it was having on me until years later.

By now I lived on my own: no roommates and no boyfriends. I was tired of living with other people. There was never any consistency with people sticking around my entire life. Then my mom ended up getting arrested and the kids were taken into foster care. I decided I would take two of my siblings in to live with me, then raise money to get a bigger house to get the rest of them. I wanted to be the savior. That was easier in thought than in practice, however. The local news station came out and tried to support what I was attempting to do. Selling candles and chocolate wasn't going to raise enough money for me to get a home for myself and six children, however. You see, by this time, my mom had given birth to ten children. The youngest one was just a baby. We all were split up, and the youngest ones I had never lived with. We older siblings did our best to help out, but we were kids ourselves.

9
Happily Ever After

I worked at the manufacturing and distribution company for eight months before I finally decided to go on a date with Jay. I remember the first time I ever went to his mom's house; I locked my keys in my car. That was embarrassing. We got along well. We drank and played video games. We had a great time together. Before you knew it, we were in a serious relationship, found out we were pregnant, and moved in together (along with my two young brothers I had taken in). We had plans to get married when we found out we were expecting a second time. We had two healthy, beautiful girls.

My mom got a new apartment and wanted her boys back, my brothers. I told her I couldn't go back and forth; if she took the boys back, I wouldn't be able to take them back again later. It was too hard on me and the children. I also was starting my own family now. She ended up losing them again, and they went into the foster care system. I was disheartened by it but felt my hands were tied. Till this day, I wish I could have kept them.

My new husband and I bought a house. We really were living what I would have called "success" at that time. We went to Jamaica for our wedding and honeymoon. That was the first time I ever left the country. I didn't go on vacations as a child. The closest thing I had to a vacation were the few times I went to church camps with my aunt's Seventh-day Adventist church. Now we made a tradition of going on a vacation every year as a married couple. Sometimes we invited his mother and my brother and would get a nice hotel suite at Myrtle Beach, South Carolina. Going on vacations added to my feeling of "finally making it to success."

One time my best friend in high school took me to Walt Disney World with her mom on a work trip. That trip actually was how my foster mom got me to stop the bulimia behaviors of binging and purging. She said that I had to stop if I wanted to go on this vacation with my friend and her mom. So I did. I stopped forcing myself to vomit after eating long enough to go on this vacation. The thing about bulimia is, when you force purge for so long, you damage your esophagus so much so that it automatically reacts when you eat.

I had finished all my courses at the community college at Harrisburg Area Community College and was now pursuing a bachelor's degree in criminal justice at Kaplan University. I worked at an inpatient psychiatric hospital for children and adolescents, but it was hard since I also was a young mom. I really wanted to stay home with my babies and give them the parenting I never got to experience. So, I started a certified home daycare. I developed an early education curriculum and a business plan and really enjoyed doing it. I could guarantee my daughters were safe, and at the same time I could help protect other people's precious children.

Becoming a mother was the most amazing thing that ever happened to me. My babies were so perfect. Everything about them amazed me. I could just stare at them and be fulfilled. It was like I finally did something right. I finally accomplished something that would sustain me forever. I thought for sure that having children would save me from my past and myself. I thought my children would be my motivation for never becoming depressed ever again. I thought I would never suffer from suicidal ideation ever again. That's what I believed.

I became a foster parent with my husband when we were caring for my brothers, and after they went back with my mom, we took in other kids who were in the foster system. So, my daughters began their first years of life with lots of kids around. The house was filled with laughter and joy. I was quite proud of myself; I had become everything I was never taught to be. I stayed up late doing my classes for college and got up way early in the morning for children to be dropped off. My house was always spotless: the dishes washed and the laundry folded. We entertained on the weekends and everything appeared perfect.

My now ex-husband has his own story to tell, so I will not go into details here. However, I did have a role in what happened. I will tell you that today we have an amazing relationship. I also have a good relationship with his mother and his girlfriend. There has been forgiveness and healing on both sides, and it is beautiful that we can successfully co-parent our daughters together.

But back then our "perfect" life began falling apart. No one knew—not even my best friends. It had to be a secret. I felt responsible. You see, a silent but deadly killer named *alcoholism* crept into our marriage. Alcoholism ultimately killed our marriage. My husband drank regularly after work and on the weekends. Sometimes I would join in; sometimes I was annoyed that it was a part of our life. I had been aware for a long time of the effects of alcoholism; after all, I grew up with it. I kept thinking that maybe I was making a bigger deal of his drinking than I should. But then there came times when he didn't know who I was while under the influence of alcohol. He grew combative and argumentative. As a result, I withdrew into that passive role I was raised to have, the one I used just to survive. I became submissive. I simply attempted to get him into a safe place so he could go to sleep. I knew that when he woke up, he would be back to himself and be remorseful. I knew it wasn't him. I knew it was the disease. He constantly minimized what happened when he was intoxicated because he couldn't remember what took place. Unfortunately, I couldn't get him to see the problem until it was too late. Eventually, I couldn't take it anymore.

I did not want to break my family apart. I tried so hard to keep us together. In order to tolerate dealing with this disease, I started drinking myself. Drinking became a daily thing. Before you knew it, we were splitting a 24 or 30 pack every night after working all day. Fortunately, this habit was short-lived; I realized that I hated who I was becoming and was not proud of the mother, wife or person I was. I had a nervous breakdown and ended up in the psychiatric hospital again. If you are counting, this was the third inpatient psychiatric stay. I was devastated that I was again in the hospital wanting to die. I thought this part of my life was over. I had been certain of it! Nevertheless, here I was.

We tried therapy as a couple, and I gave an ultimatum. Unfortunately, people can't stop doing something they feel they don't have a problem with. So, I made my husband leave. Then I rebounded from one unhealthy relationship to another, trying to fill the hole inside me that kept growing bigger—a hole that had been there from as early as I can remember. I couldn't comprehend why things were always falling apart and not working out. I look back and I see that I was addicted to chaos and people with narcissistic (selfish, controlling and manipulative) characteristics, just like my parents. Those types of relationships were what I knew and what I thought I deserved.

I ended up in these types of relationships without even being consciously aware of it. I needed to worry about someone else—anyone else—just so I didn't have to look at my own insecure self. I never realized how beautiful and intelligent I was. I never gave myself a break; I constantly belittled and doubted myself and my worth. It was *my job* to make sure everyone else was doing okay; it didn't even matter if I had just met you or if you were a long-time friend or family member. I was there for you. But this need spiraled into a cycle of trying to help or save others, to bitterness at their lack of appreciation, then to guilt for putting myself in that position (depression). I didn't care that guys used me as long as my emotional void was filled and I wasn't alone, even if just for a moment.

As soon as my husband was out the door, I was making plans for someone else to come and be with me. The thought of being alone petrified me. I flew an old friend in from California; we had dated in high school. I quickly became pregnant with my son, and I soon remembered how different the two of us were. We tried to make it work, but we were water and oil. I had so much shame that I was pregnant and not even divorced. My husband wasn't too happy, either. My husband and I tried to make it work at one point and moved back in with each other, but we quickly realized there was too much unforgiveness that we couldn't let go of at the time. Still, he came to the hospital when I gave birth to my son, and from the hospital I went back to our home. We tried living in the same house without being together, but it was just too painful for the both of us.

In the end, he wanted the house. When we bought the house, the real estate agent said we could get a better deal if my husband was on the mortgage by himself since his credit was better than mine. I didn't want to fight over the house or money, so I just left. By this point our joint bank account was drained by him, and I was left with nothing. I was really depressed. The children and I moved into a house I rented.

10
God Pull

I was so angry with God. Why would He do this? I thought if He was real, then He was mean. I didn't deserve any of this! How could this much torture come to an innocent child? Why, no matter how hard I tried, couldn't I get my life together?

I always had felt a pull toward church and God, even though I wasn't raised in any kind of religious atmosphere. I actually was raised in dozens of atmospheres—none of them with consistency—so I was just very confused. I went to the Seventh-day Adventist church with my aunt. When I lived with my dad, I used to sneak over to the Catholic church across the street. I even tried to get myself baptized using a forged note from my father! (I used forged notes a lot to get what I wanted.) In the one foster home I lived in at nine years old, I attended church with them. While in my foster home as a teen, I attended mass at the Catholic church with them. I always felt like an outsider, never a part of it. I sat on the sidelines wondering why I wasn't invited to be part of it. I remember thinking it was a "members' only" club that I just wasn't invited to. Even in the midst of all these circumstances, I felt pulled by God. I went to all kinds of services at Christian churches, Catholic churches and even a Jewish synagogue.

I remember one time when my foster mother took me to a Catholic healing service, I felt what I now know is the Spirit of God. I felt warm and tingly, like I was out of my body. I remember often crying during the church services I attended—crying about all the pain I had endured.

When I worked as a receptionist at the manufacturing and distribution company, a co-worker there was a Christian. As I remember, he always was shining, always positive, grateful and encouraging. He constantly had good advice to share. It annoyed me and drew me at the same time. It was so bizarre to me that he had lived this rough life yet shined like the sun. I had met a lot of other "Christians," but this man, as I realized later, was a true follower of Jesus.

When I was pregnant with my first daughter, I thought about what a good mother did. I didn't have any experience to compare to from my own parents, so I looked at other influential people who had come in and out of my life. Going to church was one of those things that good mothers did. So, I started attending church. I even got all three of my kids dedicated when they were born. I also got baptized when Chloe got dedicated at just six weeks old. Nothing changed, though. *Nothing*.

I tried so hard to do all the right things. I was not mentored or taught how to be a follower of Jesus. No one talked to me about having an intimate relationship with God. "Just go to church and do the right thing." That didn't seem to fit in with what I needed. I often felt let down by going to church. Nothing seemed different when I went, other than during that hour or two I was there.

11
Are We at Rock Bottom Yet?

I felt like a failure. Everything I touched seemed to turn to trash. Toward the end of my marriage I had to close my daycare and stop being a foster parent. Everything was falling apart. I didn't have much faith that I would ever have a good life.

I went and got a job in my field. I still took college courses this whole time and had finished my bachelor's degree in criminal justice. I began working on my master's in psychology; my study focus was applied behavioral analysis. I got a job as a therapeutic support staff member (TSS) and worked with children on the autism spectrum and with children with behavioral issues. During the summer I helped run a summer program in a nearby town while during the school year I worked one-on-one with children in the field, which included their homes, schools and community settings. I designed treatment plans to help meet their needs and helped them implement those plans in the home, school and community. We all need consistency.

I really enjoyed this job and believed that I was making a difference. Still, it was hard being away from my children and having someone else care for them. I had a nanny who came into our home to help ensure their environment wasn't changed too much. Then I enrolled them in an at-home daycare similar to the one I had when I ran a daycare. Still, I always was fearful that someone would hurt them.

One day in August I went to work with a child who was at a daycare center. My own children were with the sitter. (Dekan was seven months old, Kaydee was five years old, and Chloe was six.) I had been working with this particular child for only a few weeks. I remember it was a hot summer day. We were outside at the daycare; the children were enjoying what was called "splash day," where the children could play in sprinklers.

That morning the child disclosed to me that she was being sexually abused by her mom's boyfriend. As a mandated reporter, I called Children and Youth Services immediately. They came out to the daycare and interviewed the child. Then they left to go interview the child's mom and the mom's boyfriend.

I remember feeling sick to my stomach over the details of what the child disclosed to me. I tried to make sure she enjoyed the rest of her day to the best of my ability. The child had some behavioral issues and was diagnosed on the autism spectrum with verbal delays.

At one point, while playing in the water, she took off and ran indoors. I ran in after her. She was dripping water since she had been jumping and running through the sprinkler, so as she ran, she left a trail of water behind her. I got halfway across the room when I slipped and fell—*BAM!*—cracking my back and head on the floor. It rocked me! I jumped back up, a little disoriented, and wiped myself off.

I went into the bathroom and looked myself over. My back had some scrapes and I was bleeding slightly, but otherwise I physically looked okay. I was sore and had a slight headache, but I didn't feel like I had any huge injuries.

I called my work and reported it. They told me to fill out a report and asked if I felt I needed medical treatment. If I did, I was to go to their doctor's office at WORKNET. I felt I was okay. Besides, I knew that if I left, so would my client. Because she was labeled as needing one-on-one therapy, she could not be around other children without having a support staff. I had not heard back from Children and Youth Services regarding their finding, and I couldn't stomach the idea that she would have to go home. I took that word from God that I got when I was a child that I would be "a safe haven" for His children very seriously.

My work also advised me that if my symptoms got worse, to seek medical treatment. Now, I was never big on doctors. I wasn't raised getting checkups and seeking medical treatment. I always thought they were a scam.

It wasn't long till I started getting dizzy and confused. I had the symptoms of a concussion. I don't remember leaving my work. In fact, the next thing I remember, I am at the hospital. Later I was told that I called my children's fathers and told them to pick up the kids because I was going to the doctor. Apparently, I drove myself to WORKNET, a 25-minute drive, then collapsed once I made it through the doors. They transported me to the hospital by ambulance.

At the hospital, I got all the tests: MRI, CAT scans, etc. I had no identification with me, and I didn't know who I was. All I could remember was a telephone number for them to call. I didn't regain awareness of who I was until my emergency contact, my foster sister, showed up. Her arrival jogged my memory. Once I knew who I was (I was experiencing amnesia), they sent me home with a lot of medication and follow-up appointments. They told me they couldn't tell how long it would take my brain to heal or how severe the damage was. They simply told me to seek medical treatment if things worsened. *Every day* I kept feeling worse and would end up back at the hospital or at the doctors' office. It was so discouraging that I was worsening daily instead of healing.

I had suffered a concussion to the extent that it caused post-concussion syndrome (which I didn't know even existed), and I was no longer able to work. The doctor said the blow was hard enough to cause a concussion comparable to that of an athlete. I was damaged. The intellectual, physical and neurological parts of my brain were affected. Post-concussion syndrome is a complex disorder in which various symptoms last for an unidentified amount of time. The symptoms include daily chronic migraine, dizziness, shortness of breath, loss of balance, difficulty walking, psychological symptoms and cognitive issues that, in turn, include short-term memory loss and difficulty concentrating. I also developed seizures and a postural tremor. I had to use a walker to get out of bed and move around. I couldn't remember even the simplest of things; I was in constant physical and mental pain. I felt like I was being punished for something.

I was put on bed rest. I officially felt like a failure. If I couldn't take care of my children, then I was nothing. I was still grieving the finalization of my divorce that had happened just a few months prior. Now I am being told that I am permanently disabled? My work gave me workers' compensation for two months, then decided to deny it. They said I had improper footwear when I got injured. People advised me to file a lawsuit, but that's never been who I was. I met with attorneys, but I was just so exhausted from fighting all the problems life was throwing at me that I didn't want to fight anymore. It also was hard to sue; I was advised that it would be difficult because I was not on my work's property and because "slip and falls" were hard to sue for. Besides, lawyers just reminded me of the trial I had endured with my dad and I didn't want to do it. I just didn't have it in me.

As a result, I filed for Social Security Disability. I was told that I would be denied the first time, but that I would get it on the appeal. It took me 18 months to get any of that money. Needless to say, I went from a two-income household, owning my own daycare, being a foster parent, earning both of my degrees, to being divorced, broke, and jobless for 18 months. I had no support system. My foster mom died when I was 20 years old. I still didn't have a close relationship with my family. Most of my friends disappeared during my separation and divorce because they couldn't understand what happened. I learned the hard way that keeping family secrets has you losing people in the end. Here I was, trying to protect people, and I got left at the end. Even some of my own family members sided with my ex-husband because they couldn't believe he could do the things I was saying he did. That hurt a lot. So, I will end this chapter with a question: What would you do, were you in my shoes?

12
Gone, But Still Here

Back during the stress of my separation and divorce, I started seeing a doctor for migraines that I began experiencing. My family doctor tried multiple medications, none of which worked, and eventually put me on an opiate, Vicodin®. It is a narcotic. It was supposed to be a short-term fix until the doctor could find the cause of the migraines. My doctor sent me to a neurologist to try to find a solution. Between the mental health diagnosis and the medications for the migraines, I felt like a guinea pig.

The Vicodin®, however, was love at first dosage. I noticed my migraine was gone and I felt "happy." I experienced this euphoric feeling; I had energy and life in me once again. I could dance with my children even though I was sad and in so much pain. It made me feel like I did naturally before all this horrible stuff happened. Then these horrible rebound migraines hit whenever the dosage wore off. So, the doctor upped my frequency of dosage. If you had asked me at the time if I felt addicted, I would have said absolutely not. I felt like I was surviving. I would sneak an extra pill some days when I really needed to get things done around the house or when I just wanted to be able to be a mother and not stay in bed all day.

The doctor also upped my benzodiazepines multiple times since he initially had put me on them at age 17. Benzodiazepines, more commonly known as benzos, are used for anxiety and panic attacks. They work in the central nervous system and act as a tranquilizer. Some commonly known benzos are Valium®, Xanax®, Ativan® and Klonopin®. One thing that is not talked about often is how highly addictive these medications are and how they are one of two types of drugs that withdrawal from can actually kill you. Alcohol is the other. None of this was discussed with me, and I went from 0.5 mg twice a day, to 2 mg every four hours. When things got bad—which happened frequently by then—I would throw about six pills (2 mgs each) in my mouth, chew and swallow. That is 12 mg in a dosage. The side effects to the benzos that I felt were drowsiness, confusion, blackouts and impaired coordination. I loved that it made me numb. I didn't want to feel. I didn't want to feel *anything*. I would almost feel like I was dead but just aware of still being in my body. Even my body was numb. It gave me the same feeling that you feel when you are outside of your body.

When I initially was prescribed the benzos, I just trusted that the doctor knew what he was doing. I didn't know to ask questions. I was aware I was predisposed to alcoholism, but I had no idea how I would respond to addictive medications. And, as I said, I didn't know it was addictive until I was on them for over a decade!

I was angry and embarrassed that I got injured, but again I didn't see what the situation was doing to me. My self-hatred was turning into an even bigger monster. My post-traumatic stress disorder (PTSD) had become complex. So far, I had endured my mother abandoning me, being separated from my siblings, my father abusing me and going through the trial with him because of the sexual abuse, my separation and divorce, and now my work-related injury that caused me to become disabled at 29 years old.

Some of the effects of the PTSD were night terrors, avoidance, disassociation, panic attacks, extreme anger, depression, hopelessness, suicide ideation and extreme mood swings. I had experienced all these symptoms before, but not to this level. I didn't believe there was any way to come back from this. A desperation of hopelessness gripped me and really had me wanting to tap out. I wanted to throw in the towel for good. Dealing with years upon years of suicide ideation is exhausting. Fighting daily to want to even try to stay alive is a daunting task.

I felt so badly for my children. I felt sad that I had brought them into this cruel world. I felt so selfish, and I was—I was selfish for wanting to give up.

I was putting in my body, at one point, 31 prescribed pills. I think back to that time now and I believe my body didn't have a chance to heal because of the number of drugs going into it. I went to so many different doctors and specialists, always leaving with different scripts from each. I truly don't remember a lot of the next few years of my life. I have medical records and other written documents to help me put the pieces together, along with the bits that I do recall.

I don't remember this, but I was told that I posted something on Facebook about wanting to die. Someone reached out to me. I had known Kyle from high school, but we were never really friends. He said he wanted to help me. He came and stayed at my house to help me take care of the children and the house. He ran errands and helped with the day-to-day stuff. He had feelings for me, but the Lisa he met at that time wasn't even me. It was the shell of the person I once was. I felt like an old, sick, near-to-death individual living in the body of a 29-year-old. I was skin and bones, probably weighing no more than 92 pounds. I was frail and brittle and always covered in bruises just from getting up and down out of bed. Everything hurt all the time.

Kyle had survived a coma and was himself on a large amount of medication. He carried a tackle box of drugs, like a pharmacist. It contained a lot of opiates. He thought he was helping me, when I was in pain, to put a Fentanyl patch on me or give me a few pills—all on top of the crazy number of drugs I already was taking. That's not to mention that I drank and smoked weed regularly during this time as well. I had no value or respect for my life. I also had no idea what I was doing to myself.

In November of 2012, a year after my concussion, I ended up in the psychiatric hospital: fourth psychiatric hospital stay; third time at the same location. It was 14 years since my first stay there, and I felt like things were only worse, not any better. I knew the routine and went through the motions, but I left there the same as I went in: without hope.

There was one thing I left the psychiatric hospital with that I hadn't gone in with: Kurt. I knew he was bad. I could see it all over him. He was dangerous. And yet, he made me feel alive, for just a little bit. He was military, younger than me by five years, and tatted up. He was cocky and arrogant. I had no way of seeing the abuse from Kurt that was about to begin. As Kurt had been in the military, he knew how to brainwash, manipulate and control people. He was really narcissistic. Kurt also was charming and lovable at the same time. It made no sense, but my feelings for him were real at the time. I never realized I was a rescuer, thinking I could "save" other people when they didn't want saving, they wanted enabling.

I got out of the hospital right before Thanksgiving Day, and he convinced me to sneak benzos in for him and put them inside his Bible during our visit on Thanksgiving Day. He also convinced me that I should let him come stay with me when he got out. I told him I could not; that wasn't doable. The next thing I know, Kyle and I were going to pick him up when he got released from the psychiatric hospital. Before I knew it, I was asking Kyle to leave and having Kurt stay.

I am not a naïve person, but Kurt really had me. I had become a puppet for him. In retrospect, I think he had it all planned out. I was a vulnerable, lonely girl who needed saved, but it was me who was always trying to save him.

Between the divorce and the head injury, I felt like a failure as a mother, wife and provider. My attempted suicide at that time had put me in my fourth psychiatric hospital stay. Dozens of my earlier attempts went without any help because the adults in my life looked the other way. They ignored the overdoses, starvation, strangulation and slit wrists. I had given up. It felt like God, my family and the rest of the world had abandoned me, but it was I who abandoned myself.

Kurt, however, changed my world first by telling me everything I wanted to hear and by being fascinating and intriguing, then by terrorizing and threatening my life. Dealing with him depleted my energy to the point where I endured more physical and mental-health problems. I ended up in the hospital multiple times during the length of our relationship. By the time I was finished with Kurt, I was in even worse condition then when I started.

I felt like I had no choices. I was in the hospital for not being able to keep any food down. My stress and nerves were literally starting to kill me. The medical staff did an endoscopy and colonoscopy and found that I had no lining to my stomach. Between the number of drugs I put into my system for medical reasons, recreational reasons and suicide attempts, and all the stress I was enduring continuously for two decades, my stomach lining was eaten away. So, they gave me more medications just so I could keep food down and not have a burning sensation in my stomach all the time! Even while I was in the hospital, Kurt called me to see if I knew how to get gas money because he was out—let alone that he was driving my vehicle! He wasn't calling to see if I was okay or if he could come visit me. This was literally the kind of toxic stress I was in at all times.

I didn't realize it, but Kurt was crushing drugs and putting them into my drinks. As a result, I would be in and out for days. I didn't understand what was happening. One time we were arguing, and he knocked my daughter's picture off the wall. I was so angry that I started a fight over the picture. I picked up the glass in one hand while he grabbed the other side of the glass. We both got stabbed. His cut was bad enough to go to the ER by ambulance. When he called for me to pick him up, I said, "No, you can't come back here." He said, "All right, bitch, I got you." Next thing I know, the cops are at my house and having simple assault charges pressed against me. Those charges eventually got dropped because he never showed up for court.

Whenever I left the house, Kurt gave me a time limit or told me of the consequences for leaving. He followed through with those consequences. One time, he beat our family dog. When I came home, I found a trail of blood through the house, patches of dog fur all over, and my daughter's doll house smashed up. The back sliding door was wide open, and Kurt wasn't there. I thought the dog was dead and fell on the floor wailing. I called 911. Fortunately, they found Buddy a few days later; my ex-husband came and took him to a farm. The dog was originally my ex-husband's. I can still remember the sick feeling I had in my stomach.

I used to be one of those people who didn't understand why women stayed in unhealthy, abusive relationships. But you don't know what you don't know, until you know. I couldn't believe what I had tolerated for most of my life. Yet, what was the alternative? What were my choices? I didn't feel as if I had any.

I wrote this poem at the beginning of our relationship. It shows the level to which I was being manipulated. I looked to him as a savior, and he all but killed me.

"Poetry of a Lost Girl by Me"

When the rain looks like it's never going to stop,
And the sun will never come out again.
When the world is spinning way too fast,
And you wish you could get off.
When death feels like your only option,
But you're too scared to succeed.
When you ask God why you have been punished
And you get no reply.
When you feel like it's your fault
But yet you did nothing wrong.
Out of nowhere comes the sun and the world will slow down.
An angel is sent to me and the meaning of life is now so clear.
God has sent me you to take away my pain
and bring only happiness.
You are the reason I smile and the reason I cry.
I hope this feeling never goes away.
I feel like this is something I could hold on to forever.
I pray that you are never taken away from me and you have
no need to leave.
You are the only one for me!

13
Losing Myself

I thought I had things under control, even though that meant the rest of the world had gone mad. I simply was trying to survive and live in a selfish, manipulative world of liars and con artists. My thoughts were comprised of such wonderings as, *What have I done? Why did I bring kids into this madness that I can't control?* So many fingers pointed at me, blaming me for so many things—and most of the fingers came from my own hands. I thought others' feelings were my responsibility, even if I didn't cause those feelings. Honestly, I had spiraled out of control, and the longer I stayed in this mind-set, the worse it became.

I personally struggled more with the "taking care of myself" part. I knew for certain that if I went to my doctors, took my medication as directed, and looked after everyone else, then my happiness somehow would emerge magically. That was a stupid thought. No one can be happy when she sacrifices her own happiness for others all the time! When you constantly go through the cycle of helping others (which makes you feel good), but they don't reciprocate the thoughtfulness (which makes you sad and feel abandoned and used), then you succumb to resentment and anger (which comes from being used and feeling empty) and that's when depression kicks in. When you find someone new to help, you become distracted from your existing problems and instead you find new hope in "saving" someone else. It is a vicious cycle that doesn't end until you've had enough of being used and have nothing but a bunch of needy, selfish people in your life. In short, sometimes you have to hit bottom.

You can listen to the facts and sayings about life and happiness and recovery and moving on, but until you're ready, you will continue to live in this codependent state of mind that hears only what it wants to hear. It is crazy the amount of pain we can put ourselves through with no one to justly blame for it but ourselves. Because of our thoughts and how we react to them, we just don't see things that way at the time. This cycle is painful, devastating and draining. It sucks away all of your energy, appreciation and sanity. It truly drives you insane, slowly but surely, until you either snap and do something you regret for the rest of your life, or you stop and realize who and what you are and make changes to become the person you want to be, the person you truly are but lost somehow along the way. You don't even know how it all happened, but more importantly, you don't know what to do about it now.

The thoughts we had as children, innocent and sweet, but determined and motivated, is what we must find again. We need to get back the innocence and simplicity of childhood, the motivation and drive to conquer the world like a champion, and the ability to pat ourselves on the back and say, "Job well done! Never knew I had that in me!"

I thought I had everything under control. Then, my life came to a screeching halt when my world tumbled from underneath me again. I didn't want to go to the hospital because I knew the routine. I had my master's degree in psychology, for goodness' sake. Yet, I was never able to help myself. I wanted to die, but I didn't want to leave my children motherless. If I stayed with this man who ruined my life but whom I still loved (was infatuated with), I felt I would be abandoning my children. Neither could I go to the hospital and expect them to automatically fix me. It didn't work the other four times, and it wasn't going to work now. *I* needed to do the work. *I* needed to do my own recovery. *I* needed to get my depressed butt out of bed and make something of my life.

Where did my goals go? Where were my morals and values? Everything had been sacrificed. I was left to deal with it alone because I knew that *I* was the only one who could save me. I was so sick of living a life in this pattern of victim to rescuer, of anger to revenge or lashing out, then depression.

It is not our job to make people feel a certain way. We have to learn to live through our emotions in a positive way, using coping skills and a good support system, not by self-blaming, belittling others, contemplating whether to live or not, or whether or not to run away as fast as we can! I have felt and thought all of these. We can't use our emotions as a justification to do whatever we want. Rather, we must realize that our choices have consequences and that those consequences will make things harder, not easier. It's not until we stop making the poor choices and deal with the consequences that we can move into seasons of reaping good. Too often we want instant gratification, and when it doesn't happen, we stop the "good" we were doing and fall back to making poor choices—the very things that usually cause all the crisis in our lives in the first place.

When my life with Kurt shattered on Easter morning in 2013, I had had enough! It was like the lights went on in my head and I saw how to handle this situation and my life in general. It wasn't going to be easy, but it was doable. This time, with my eyes wide open, I was able to go through my recovery cycle without attempting suicide. I *was* suicidal for a week or two, but slowly I started enjoying life again. I chose to start loving myself the way I loved others—to respect and treat myself the way I treated others. This was not a quick fix. I had to be patient with myself to grieve for *all* the pain I had suffered in my life. I had to deal with the repressed memories. I had to learn to forgive but not forget. I realized I was okay just the way I was. I didn't have to let people trample on me, then turn around and blame myself for their using me. I didn't have to lash out due to an overload of unfinished business.

Today, I am proof that the lost can be found, that the living dead can be reborn into life and have a second chance. Don't get caught up in regretting how much of your life you spent living the wrong way; just think positive, be optimistic and surround yourself with good people and things. It took me till I was 32 years old to figure it out. At first, I was disappointed that it took me so long to comprehend what the counselors and psychiatrists had been telling me since I was 15. But guess what? It is better late than never! My glass is half full, not half empty anymore. I can hold up my head without getting nervous that someone will make eye contact with me and see my pain and my fears and use them against me, like I let Kurt and so many others do. Kurt knew I was very vulnerable, and he was in a situation where he needed someone else to take on his baggage because he couldn't and wouldn't deal with it.

In 2012, a counselor asked me if I "treat others the way I treat myself." I corrected her and said, "Isn't it 'treat others how you want to be treated'?" She said, "Yes, that is true, but would you ever be as hard on someone else as you are on yourself?" I sat there pondering it for a while, and it sunk in: I expected myself to be better than everyone else and to take the blame when things fell apart.

On April 26, 2013, I emailed my pastor and loved ones who were trying to reach me. I was too sad to talk, so I emailed, texted and messaged those who reached out to me. This was an important step since I had a history of isolating when I was suffering. I finally had realized that I can't hide from the world; it's still out there whether I want it to be or not. So, I finally reached out to a few people.

From: Lisa
To: Pastor
Sent: Friday, April 26, 2013
Subject: Hi, it's Lisa…

Pastor,

Thanks for checking on me. I really need your prayers and support. I would call, but it's hard to talk without crying right now. I'm not sure how much I have shared with you, if anything, but in November of 2012 I met Kurt. He was having problems with his mental health, and so was I. When I met him, I knew right away that I loved (was infatuated with) him and was supposed to help "save him" from his addictions and PTSD from his military tours. I asked God many times if this is what I was supposed to do. All signs showed me "yes" and, oh boy, was I deceived. I took Kurt (who was homeless at the time) into my house, basically as a stranger. Slowly but surely, I started seeing the lies, betrayal, usage of my car, money and anything else he could get, he stole from me, and I repeatedly forgave him, blaming his addiction and listening to his lies of how he was going to get sober for me. I knew he wanted to get better, but his addiction had a hold of him. He has mentally and emotionally abused me, he has threatened me, stole from me many times, damaged my vehicle when high on drugs, fed me lines of how he loved me more than drugs, he made my kids uneasy (which I didn't know at the time or was in denial about, not sure), he made me a prisoner in my own life (I wasn't allowed to make my own decisions anymore because he was in charge of me). I was blindsided by my love for him and desire to help him get sober for himself, his son and me. I broke up with him many times, but he wouldn't accept it. He controlled my phone, who I talked to and what I said. He was hospitalized three times since I met him six months ago, and in jail twice, but my heart wouldn't accept the facts that he didn't want to get better, or not bad enough.

On Easter morning at 3 a.m. he broke into my new residence, causing damage to the property I am renting, and I awoke to him towering over my bed. He kept me and my son in the house and wouldn't let me leave or call anyone unless it was on speaker phone. When he had to use the bathroom, I quickly messaged a friend who already knew my address and told them to call the police. He has been in jail since a few days after that. I got granted a three-year PFA (protection from abuse) on Monday for me and my kids with no contact by him, but it's just a piece of paper. I had court today with him but didn't find out till the last minute, but I couldn't mentally handle it because I was not prepared and I have been depressed, anxious and sometimes suicidal since the incident.

I accept who he is, but I am angry that I loved someone who only loved himself and drugs. I was used over and over and have turned my life upside down trying to help someone, and I was the one hurt in the end.

I am confused. Is this the work of God or the devil? I thought I was doing the right thing, like usual, and then I get screwed. I blame myself for my stupidity. People tried to warn me, but I didn't accept what they said. Now he will be in jail for some time for robbery, breaking and entering, false imprisonment, harassment, stalking, and many more violations of the law against me. I know I am doing the right thing, but why am I so negative and blaming myself?

I need to be positive for myself and my kids. I take on the problems of the world and feel like I'm drowning. Thanks for checking on me especially when I am down, depressed and not wanting to live…but I want to change this thought process. I am doing a lot of self-help and am signed up for counseling for me and the kids. Hope all is well and sorry I couldn't call. I appreciate you and the church in my life. Any advice would be helpful. I am confused if this is the doing of God or the devil or neither?

God Bless,
Lisa

From: Pastor
To: Lisa
Sent: Monday, April 29, 2013
Subject: Re: Hi, it's Lisa ...

Hi Lisa,

I am sorry I didn't get a chance to email sooner. I am sorry as well that you had to go through everything as you conveyed in your email. It is difficult to say if it is the work of God or the work of the devil. Maybe a little bit of both. My advice would be to simply focus on your health and well-being first off so that you can get to a good place in your life where you can share it with some-one else. You need to be healthy so that you can take care of your children. I understand that you want to "save" others, but that is not your responsibility. That is God's. And, yes, each one of us is called to help others, but that shouldn't mean that you jeopardize your life, your family, your home, etc. It is important to maintain good, healthy boundaries. You need to be a good example to your children, which starts off with helping them see you as a healthy individual. If you need to talk, please feel free to call me. In the meantime, you and your family are in my prayers.

Peace,
Pastor

From: Lisa
To: Pastor
Sent: Monday, April 29, 2013
Subject: RE: Hi, it's Lisa...

Thanks, Pastor...

Your response has been the best advice I've received. I didn't re-alize that I put my life and my kids out of my sight because I was so focused on "rescuing" Kurt. I realized I have codependency and need to gain control back in my life. I was suicidal till three days ago. I am still depressed, but my eyes are open. I see that I was used and misused for as much as I would give, and since I was already low in life, it took my focus off my own problems. I am thankful for all the positive things in my life. I have healthy kids who are wonderful. I have a house, food, clothes and money for me and my kids. I have a car to get them to school and where they need to get and me to my doctor appointments (which I have been ignoring)....

I know I can recover from this. This is not the first or last time that a life lesson has come my way; it's just going to be a year or so till all the court hearings and trial is over with Kurt. He is looking at some serious time for what he did. He did come to church once, but I don't know if you met him. Anyway, I have dealt with death, divorce, financial struggles, almost being homeless and without food, without a vehicle, and all my child-hood abuse and neglect, and I'm still here! I put my faith in God that He is watching over me and my kids. I really need prayers for my physical and mental health. Thanks, and God bless you and your family. You are a blessing in my life.

Lisa

I want to end this chapter by saying that although I went to church oc-casionally, talked about God, and so forth, I did not have a relationship with God. I also did not have salvation. Don't be confused; going to church or doing any such routine does not cause your life to change or alter. I had got-ten to the point of self-help, but it is temporary and will not sustain lasting, permanent change. Rather, there needs to be a surrendering to God, accept-ing Jesus as your Lord and Savior, repenting of your sins, turning away from them and living a different life. You also need to have the Holy Spirit come dwell inside of you. God designed us for this. All are welcome to His family! You *are* invited to this "club"!

14
The Economic Impact

Remember that concussion? It took 18 months of waiting before my Social Security Disability kicked in. I injured my head in August of 2011 but didn't start receiving benefits until January of 2013. Meanwhile, I was living on welfare, county assistance and child support, and together it covered less than half of our expenses. As a result, I was left coming up with over a thousand dollars more per month for 18 very long months. We went without heat during the winter of 2012. We had a space heater, and the kids and I all slept in my bed. We always had food because of food stamps, but I could never get on housing assistance because the waiting list was so long. People helped as they could, giving us a hundred here and a hundred there.

It was exhausting, asking for help. I grew up being taught not to depend on anyone. I grew up with no support system, so I didn't have people to depend on. There was no one for me to move in with or anyone to take the burden off me.

It is of the utmost importance that you understand the desperation a person in a crisis situation (which is exhausting in itself) feels when trying to get help and having every door slammed on her (or him). Such a case causes a whole other level of defeat. You literally feel like you are drowning. Every day you are just barely treading water. Sometimes it gives you peace to think that if you just stop trying, it could all be over.

I daydreamed about death like most would a vacation. Going on a vacation was too farfetched of an idea for me at this point; death, however, seemed right around the corner. With death, there would be no more suffering or pain...no more torment of trying to survive...no more trying to convince someone that I was worthy of his time or love...no more trying to keep people around, since I knew eventually everyone leaves. I had seen it time and time again. Even the parents who gave birth to me didn't protect and stand by me. I was the common denominator, so it had to be me. Everything I came in contact with fell apart. That's what I believed. That was the picture my circumstances painted for me. That was the lie of the enemy that I bought into my whole life. Somehow, all my circumstances were all my fault, and I could not fix anything. My body and mind were filled with anxiety, depression, pain and hopelessness.

Every month during this year and a half, I came up a little bit shorter. My landlord was not too sympathetic about my situation. Obviously, it was business to him. First, my rent was a week late. Then I went to partial payments. Before I knew it, I was three months behind and had an eviction notice. It was just about then that my disability got approved and I received my retro pay. Too bad that money was spent before I even got it. My credit was destroyed; I had so much debt that I felt I could never get out from under it. I paid what I could. I got a new apartment in an area I wouldn't normally choose to live, but the rent was more affordable. I had been paying $1,050 just for rent (utilities and oil heat were extra) for the house I had been renting. My disability check was only $772 for myself and three kids. So, I got a place where I could. I kept my ex-husband's address so the kids could continue at the school they were at and just transported them daily.

My children were my motivation for life. Every morning I had to open my safe of drugs and swallow down a whole combination just to get out of bed. These pills were not to get me high; they were to make me functional! I literally woke up and felt like my body had no life, that it had no muscle left to do simple movements. After the drugs, I got the girls ready for school, fed them and dropped them off with hugs and kisses and best wishes for their day. Then I returned home with my son, got him a sippy cup of milk, put his favorite show on the TV, and headed back to bed.

I used to have so much shame about the details of my daily life. I hated that that was where I was at. However, it was the reality of what I was living. I was staying alive only for them. I had no hope for the future. I no longer had goals or dreams. I no longer could see myself working in my field or having a safe haven for God's children. I couldn't believe how far I had fallen and how far I was from where I was headed. It seemed impossible to get back on the right track. Instead, I felt like the tracks had been removed and all I had left was this existence in which I didn't even recognize myself in the mirror. Who was this empty, broken, angry and bitter girl? I hated life. I hated myself. I just wanted this to be over already.

With the little bursts of energy I got from the opiates, I would do scrap-booking and other things with the kids. All the energy I had went to them. The scrapbooks I made were so they could remember me when I was gone. I was always planning for my death. I didn't tell people that, but that's what I was doing. I wanted them to remember all the amazing times they had with me. I wanted them to remember the fun-loving person who gave them all she could. I didn't want to be remembered as the mom who sold out and took her life selfishly, leaving them motherless.

People constantly were telling me how selfish it is to die. People used to tell me that I would go to hell if I committed suicide because God didn't for-give that sin. None of those comments help when a person is in this pain. I used to imagine myself in eternal sleep. I didn't dream of heaven or angels or gold streets. I thought of sleep. I just wanted to go to sleep and not wake up. Why is that such a big deal? I would think. It is my life. No one understands what I have been through. They don't have to feel this hurt all the time.... I don't believe God punishes people who take their lives when the pain of living is too great. God is a God who judges the heart. He loves us deeply. He sees and feels everything we do. He is not a God who punishes us because of our pain. Now, this is not an invitation for you to take your life. Keep reading. I'll explain more later.

15
The People You Meet

Everyone who was a friend was gone. Some people I alienated because I was too embarrassed of what I had become. Some left because they didn't understand or couldn't handle watching the unraveling of what I had become. I felt like I had no control over my circumstances. The types of people you attract when you are living this lifestyle are different. Instead of attending PTA meetings in the evenings, I was hosting drinking parties. It was like I reverted back to my high school years. My philosophy became, "If you can't change it, numb it!" People I hadn't seen in a decade were around. Other people who drank and partied came simply for the laughs and the party. I called them all friends, but in the morning, when reality hit, none of them were there. When life was real, none of them stayed. When it was time to party, though, they all showed up. It was high school all over again! But since I didn't like to be alone with these thoughts and with this life, I guess I believed it was better to have some friends then no friends at all. Except, I was wrong.

People who live this lifestyle motivate you to head in the opposite direction of where you should go. Their solutions to problems aren't legal or smart. Nevertheless, I took notes. I said, "Nah, that's not me. I don't do stuff like that." But before I knew it, I was selling nickel and dime bags of weed. That was too much running and fussing for just a few dollars, though, so I went to peddling pills. I wasn't going to sell any of my pills, however; I needed them for my own supply. I needed more pills, so I got with people who messed with pills. These people also dealt with heroin and meth, crack and cocaine. Every day I learned more about the drug game. I knew some stuff because as a kid I had overheard and seen things while at parties with my dad. I also learned bits and pieces from my drug-dealing friends in high school and college, but

I was never a dealer. I seldom paid for drugs in high school and college; I was a cute girl and used that to my advantage. I mostly got my recreational drugs for free or at least discounted.

Being under the influence of drugs 24/7 deteriorates your morals and values. I wasn't actually raised with many morals and values, but as a young adult and mother I had developed them. Now I was back to thinking and living the creed of "survival of the fittest." Only the strong survive. Well, my idea of how to be strong was poop. I did many things during this time that I don't remember; any memories I do have are foggy and scattered. I did things that don't line up with the character of who I am at all. As I look back, I am not sure if it was from disassociating, the concussion, the stress, the drugs or just a combination of them all, but I was doing things daily that I normally would never do.

I remember people telling me of the illegal things they did, of the crimes they committed, and I'd think, "Not me. I would never." One of the people who had stuck around for a while, whom I called my best friend, was Ty, a flamboyantly gay black guy. I considered him to be my safe person. He made me laugh when I wanted to cry. He came up with solutions when I wanted to give up, even if they weren't legal. He paraded me around in circles that made me money and introduced me to people whom I normally would never have been around.

When he introduced me to Kelly, I felt so bad for her. She had lost her kids, was addicted to heroin, and was prostituting every day just to get high. She was about ten years older than me, or at least she looked it. I remember saying out loud (but not to her), "That is the most degrading thing a person could do; I would kill myself before I would ever do that!" When she shared her story with me, I felt so much empathy for her. I wanted to help her. I tried to tell her things could be different. I gave her all this hope that I didn't even have for myself.

That was something I always did: I had hope for others but none for myself. I had to learn the hard way that people follow your actions, not your words. Kelly used to come and hang out and we talked and drank. She seemed normal; she seemed like a normal person who fell on hard times. She shared with me when her boyfriend beat her, so I invited her to come stay with me for a little while. I even was crazy enough to go and threaten her boyfriend with a taser while she got her belongings out of the house. I always intervened when there was abuse going on. I couldn't stand by and watch. I have jumped on the backs of men and attacked them just to get them to leave women alone.

Kelly would leave, go trick (prostitute), get her heroin, get high, then come back. She minimized prostitution, as if it wasn't that big of a deal. She said, "We have sex with men for free; why not get paid for it?" She started teaching me how she did it without ever standing on a corner. She taught me how to go about it without getting caught. Even when she did, it was merely a summary charge. Kelly told me how to be choosey about a clientele. As a result, I started doing my own research, but I was not convinced. I still thought it was gross and disgusting.

Financially, I was still struggling. My household was barely hanging on from month to month. I remember being so overwhelmed just buying toilet paper. I didn't have the money for this necessity, and when I bought toilet paper from the dollar store, a pack of four rolls only lasted us four days. Ugh. It was devastating. For some reason, it was that little thing that put me on edge. A person shouldn't be overwhelmed by buying toilet paper for her family. But there I was, for years worried about having toilet paper. I have to tell you that today I buy the best quality toilet paper I can find, and I have lots of it. I never worry about toilet paper today.

I got into some legal trouble over a prank that got into the wrong hands at the end of 2013. It made me look like a creep, but really it was a joke with very bad judgment. Growing up, I was around adults with crude humor all the time, some of which I had picked up. A detective came to my house. I had no idea what for and felt punched in the gut when I found out. The detective took my story and since the other person's story lined up, he was going to ask for it to be dropped to a lesser charge or dropped altogether. The charge itself would have been really bad.

While the detective was there, three of my friends were upstairs hiding in my room. Two of them had outstanding warrants. All of them were planning a trip to Florida to "make some money." I was in some serious trouble here, yet I was still trying to protect others instead of myself. The detective told me to go for pretrial and gave me all the details on what to do. Then he left.

I went upstairs and found my so-called friends had left via the back stairwell, taking with them the $2,000 in cash I had stashed in my dresser drawer. I had just finished saving that money. My engine blew in my SUV and I had saved that money to get a new vehicle. As I stood there in my bedroom, part of me snapped. I just didn't care anymore. I was going to do what I had to do to take care of my children. I was done letting people take advantage of me and pin me as the bad guy. I was sick of playing the victim. I was tired of feeling sorry for myself. I needed to take control of my life. I felt it was the only logical thing to do.

I made a Backpage account and profile. I used a different name and created a whole different persona. I used pictures that looked like me but were not me. The first thing I noticed was I got to be different, to feel different. I got an adrenaline rush being someone other than myself. I created a look for this alter ego. She looked different, talked differently, and had a different personality. I actually found it comforting to be able to get away from myself and my life and be this other person. As time went on, I built multiple different personas. I was Alexis, Natalie and Winter. For once in my life, I felt like I was in control. I made the rules. I said who could play. I decided who I was going to be. I felt like I was on top of the world.

I played games with myself; for instance, I set myself to see how much money I could make in 24 hours. Before I knew it, Lisa was hardly around anymore. When she did make an appearance, she was depressed and suicidal. I would go to calls for 24 hours straight, then crash for days. The one crucial thing I had to do in order to take on these different personalities was a lot of drugs. I started using all the street drugs. It happens so quickly. First it was just the pills for energy, the weed to calm my nerves, and the cocaine to help me feel like I owned the universe. Then, people had meth, crack and heroin and want you to do what they are doing, and you do. The truth is, when you run away from yourself, you cause so much damage to your body, mind and spirit.

I didn't recognize myself in the mirror. I felt permanently numb. I didn't take any responsibility for how I got to this point in my life. I felt like I had no choice. I simply was doing what I had to do. The thing about sexual abuse survivors is that part of them identifies with that abuse; they see it as part of who they are. I saw myself as a sexual object, and I hated it. I hated that other people during my life, four to be exact, decided what I would do and how I would do it sexually. In addition to what I have already disclosed, I was date raped twice, once when I was around 17 years old and again at 21. I felt powerless both times.

The thing about prostitution is that you get to be in control. It had been such a long time since I felt I had any control in my life. I knew that men saw me as a sex object, so why not use it to my advantage and get control back? For once *I* got to decide.

16
I Have Gone Mad

Everything I did in my life was for my children. I know that last chapter doesn't sound like it, but what I did was for them. I was willing to degrade myself and sell my body so I could provide for them. I would have done anything to keep them safe. My children have never seen me use a drug; they just knew I was sick. I protected them even from myself. I'm so thankful that I got sober before they got older, or it definitely would have affected them hardcore.

On February 3, 2014, my ex-husband found out about my legal troubles and went for temporary custody of the children. I instantly lost my whole mind. I became suicidal; I called and told him that I would kill myself if he took them from me. He called the police, and they had to break into my house to do a "welfare call." I was talking crazy. I had locked myself in the bathroom and was figuring out how to take my life before they got into the room. I didn't figure it out, and they busted in the door. I was "302'd," or involuntarily committed, for the first time and transported to Fairmount Psychiatric Hospital in Philadelphia for ten days.

All the other times I was hospitalized, people were able to convince me to go into the psychiatric ward voluntarily because it's easier to get out. This time I decided I was not having it. If I didn't have my children, then I had nothing. I was nothing. I just kept saying, "I don't care," and I meant it. I did my ten days there, then the authorities had me brought back home. I remember there was a big snow. I had worn animal slippers in the ambulance on the way, and they got soaked in the snow when they dropped me off.

I walked back into my home, and everything was just as I had left it. It was so empty without my kids in it. It wasn't even a home anymore; it was just a building I lived in. I dealt with eating disorders throughout my life, as

I discussed before, but nothing compared to what I dealt with then. I had to purchase Ensure drinks just to get some calories into my body. I weighed no more than 100 pounds and looked sick. Because of my health conditions, I had a constant tremor. Drugs made it better, I thought, but maybe I just couldn't feel it then.

I was making a lot of money, but I didn't care anymore. I created a fake cleaning business just to cover up all the money coming in. I had done it to provide for my babies, but they were gone. Now I was addicted to the game. I really had checked out; Lisa was gone. I did not do any follow-up treatment from the psychiatric hospital; neither did I take seriously any self-care. I knew what to say to the doctor to get out; besides, they can only keep you so long because of insurance policies.

Within a week of my release from Fairmount, I was planning the most serious suicide attempt yet. I bought and counted out 300 opiates. This was the end of the line for me. I had given up 100 percent. I used milk to take the pills because I knew I was less likely to vomit them up then. I had been attempting suicide with pills since I was nine years old. I felt like I was somewhat of an expert by this time, even though I was still alive. I was 32 years old now. I was so tired. The thought of dying seemed a much more peaceful choice than facing the reality of what I was living. I took all 300 pills. I sat in my bed all propped up, taking a few pills at a time. I literally took all 300 pills! But I didn't even get high or drowsy. Well, I guess I should say I didn't get any higher than I normally was.

For anyone not familiar with addiction, let me explain that the addict gets to a point where she is just getting to a baseline, not a withdrawing level. It isn't a high that is exciting anymore. It is just to not be sick.

Anyway, I didn't die. I fell asleep and woke up the next day. I felt a "gush," like I peed myself or, if I had been pregnant, like my water broke (I was *not* pregnant). When I checked myself to see what happened, I saw that all the pills, in powder form, had come out. I heard a soft voice say, "You are mine. It will not touch you." I was angry. I thought, *Why must I continue to be punished by being alive?*

17
How Could It Get Any Worse?

I continued to "escort." That is the term I liked to use. It simply is a fancy word for prostitution. Because I was so choosey about my clientele, I often was with professors and businessmen. It really wasn't about sex as much as about companionship. Yes, there were some weird and nasty requests from men sometimes, but I was not about that lifestyle and never brought myself to do any of those things.

Eventually I slipped up. I got careless because I really didn't care anymore. Every day I was just hoping I would die. I got arrested for prostitution on April 1, 2014, by an undercover detective. The police took me to booking and gave me a summary charge, just like Kelly told me would happen, and then I was released. It was the first time, as an adult, that I ever was in a booking center and had my mug shot taken. I went home and was disgusted with myself. *Who are you?* I would think to myself. I laid low for a little while, then went right back at it. I was now addicted to the game. I traveled out of the area and posted there so I wasn't getting picked up by the same detective agency doing the undercover work.

I was called out to a hotel with these guys whom I had never met before. They wanted to be my "bodyguards," otherwise known as my pimps. I laughed at them. I worked for myself. I wasn't going back under the control of a man. There was another girl there, and she appeared uncomfortable about something. I guess she was being pimped out by these guys and was not okay. I called her into the bathroom to do drugs with me, where I told her she could come stay with me and I would show her how I did things. I wanted her to be safe. I wanted her not to be under the control of these men. I wanted to save her.

She came and stayed with me for less than two weeks. I was trying to get her off opiates. She was freebasing them (smoking the pills). I now know that I was trying to redeem some of my life by helping her, but she didn't want help. For instance, she used my car to go to her parents' house, but then I found out that she really went back to the dealer/pimp. I told her if that's what she wanted, then she could leave, and I asked my friend to give her a ride. He did, and she got arrested within 12 hours. When they questioned her about who she worked for, she told them me! Why would she do that? I was of no use to her anymore. She certainly wasn't going to give up her drug dealer; she needed him. She didn't need me anymore. The girl had to give someone up, though, or she would be charged with possession, prostitution, etc. So, she said it was me. In the cops' eyes, it added up. She was staying in my house and using my car, my laptop, my bank card, etc. I looked guilty.

I had no idea that this had happened, until…

I was sitting in my bed, where I normally hung out when I was home, when I heard the loudest bang of my life. I didn't realize it, but it was my front door being knocked in. I heard an authoritative man's voice shout, "Lisa, come down with your hands up!" I had already jumped up out of bed; my entire body was convulsing. *What is going on? What do I do?* I threw a cigarette in my mouth, lit it, grabbed my purse and started running down the steps. I had moved my bedroom to the third floor since my kids weren't there anymore. I never moved so quickly in my life.

I got down to the first floor to find a dozen detectives and police officers inside my home and trailing outside the front of my house. The street was lined with police cars. I could see them because my front door had been kicked in. That was that bang. They knocked it in. I was shaking as I tried to understand what they were saying. My thoughts were frantic. *How is this happening? What is happening? Is this a nightmare?* The arresting officer stated, "You are under arrest for the promoting of prostitution and other related charges."

Whoa, hold up! What did they just say? I replayed it in my head. *I didn't do that. Speak!* I frantically started talking with my hands. I tried to explain to them what had really happened, but they didn't want to hear any of it. They asked for me to take my jewelry off and leave my purse at home. I was only allowed to bring my house key. They confiscated my phone and my laptop as evidence. I wasn't allowed to get changed. I was wearing a black camisole and cheetah-print pajamas. So that is what I went to the booking center wearing. I had no bra, no socks, just my winter boots and my pajamas.

18
Booking and Intake

I was literally in shock. How can someone just say something and it becomes truth when it isn't the actual truth? How can what I have to say not matter at all? I was handcuffed and put into the back of the cop car. All my neighbors were outside, watching. Surely things couldn't get more embarrassing than that, but they did. We got to the same booking center where I had just been 17 days earlier for the first time. *This is surreal. This cannot be really happening.* I was booked, fingerprinted and had my mug shots taken. Unlike 17 days earlier, I was then put into a holding cell and not released. I was in this white cement room for hours. I bawled the whole time. I thought my life literally was over. This was worse than death. I just kept thinking over and over how I would never see my children again. This was literally the worst day of my life. I had had a lot of bad days—some of them I talked about in this book—but this was the icing on the cake.

When they got me in front of the judge via FaceTime on a laptop, he set a $25,000 bail and said that he wanted me to sit. I looked bad. I had been charged three different times for three different things in a matter of two months. I never thought I would be in a prison—well, at least not as an inmate. I wouldn't even go visit people in prison because I was traumatized by seeing my father in prison at an early age. I didn't want anything to do with prisons.

I had gotten my degree in criminal justice and psychology to try to help the system. I wanted to understand why we did the things we do and how to change it. I did my internship at the county probation and parole office. I was one of the good guys. Or, I guess I used to think I was.

They took me over to the prison from booking. The booking center and the prison are right next to each other. I went through the questioning, the strip search, the humiliation and dehumanization, and then got my tan uniform. I was deemed as suicidal based on my answers to their questions. They were accurate with their conclusion. I was put on suicide watch in a strip cell for seven days. I couldn't even have my glasses or my shoes. It was my tan uniform, my body and a wool blanket. I couldn't even have toilet paper without asking for it.

Once they closed that prison door behind me and I was in my cell, I started hyperventilating. I literally could not get out. I was in a cell, locked in and couldn't get out. I had a full panic attack that wouldn't give up. I was screaming and crying for help, and they told me to shut up. I told them I need my medicine, my benzos, and they laughed. They said, "You won't be getting those in here, honey." Benzos are something you can die from during withdrawal. I had been pumping so many pills into my body on any given day that I knew for sure I was going to die.

I couldn't get out of this cell, so I decided to get out of this life. I was determined to find a way to kill myself in this cell. My bunk was for two people, but it was just me in the cell. On suicide watch they have you alone. There were holes on the metal on the top bunk, and I thought that if I pulled the wool blanket through that hole, maybe I could hang myself. I could easily see those holes because they keep the lights on bright, 24 hours a day, so as to see what is going on in a cell at all times. I just lay there in my bunk looking up, daydreaming about how I was going to pull off this suicide, when the most amazing thing happened.

There had been times, such as when I was six years old, when I thought I had heard the voice of God. This time, though, there was no mistaking it. God audibly spoke to me. He said, "I know you are so tired and want to come home. I have seen everything that has happened to you, and I want you to know none of it has happened for longer than it needed to for the Kingdom of heaven to come to earth through you. I have been with you the whole time. If you want to come home, I will let you. But if you let Me, I will give you a new life where these things don't happen to you anymore. I will carry you."

As He spoke this to me, I saw my children's faces. I thought about how it would cause them so much heartache to have me gone forever and about how cowardly it was of me to leave them. I said, "Okay, yes, let's do it Your way. I give You my life." In that moment, I fell to my knees. I had no idea what I was signing up for, but I was so tired of doing it my way and always wanting to die. In that moment of my surrender, everything changed. My addiction was gone. My physical ailments were gone. My suicide ideation and anxiety were gone. I had peace like I never before had experienced. I felt joy and hope and freedom. It was the most bizarre feeling to be in a prison cell and feel free.

19
Freedom

I often say that I had to go to prison to escape from prison. The truth was, I had been in prison for as long as I could recall. From a very young age, I had been in prison mentally, emotionally and spiritually. I don't believe the devil put me in jail. I believe the Lord looked at my life and said, "This is all poop." (Yes, He talks to me that way!) "Let Me put you over here where you are safe while I remove everything from your life; then we can start from scratch. You can build your foundation on Me, and I will rebuild your life."

The one thing I recall is that throughout my life I would often blame God or pray and ask Him to do something for me—change, fix or save me—or I would ask Him a question. The problem was, either I didn't know how to hear Him answer me or I was too stubborn to do things His way.

I had a worldly view of things my whole life. I had developed this entitlement mentality that something was owed to me because of what happened to me throughout my life. That thinking left me bitter and sad when things didn't magically happen as I thought they should. I justified my lifestyle of partying, drugs, alcohol and sexual promiscuity because of how I was raised. I would think, *That's nothing compared to what I have seen others do.* I was waiting to hit the lottery, metaphorically speaking, but I wasn't willing to put in the work to get there.

I thought living free meant doing what I wanted, when I wanted, and how I wanted. I thought being strong was being tough and becoming hard and cold to the world. I had developed this belief system that people in prison were bad guys, that addicts chose to get hooked, and that homeless people chose to live on the streets.

Well, this time in a cell is what I call my last semester of college. Today, I own the fact that I had no idea what I was talking about. When people use the saying, "you don't know unless you walk in their shoes," I sincerely understand that now—for I am now the one walking in those shoes that most people don't understand.

I learned more through this experience and all that came from it than in the six years I went to college. Be careful about how and what you judge because life has a way of walking you through the things you've said you'd never be. I said that I would never be an addict or a prostitute or go to prison, and now I have done all of them. I didn't have them on my bucket list or anything; rather, they were on my "not in my lifetime" list.

As much as you might think I would wish my life were different, I actually am super thankful for everything I have walked through. I would not be who I am today if I had not walked through everything and come out on the other side. And, as you will learn as you continue reading, my life is still a wild adventure every single day—just in a very different way!

Back when I was a teen, there was an activity I was made to do during therapy. I hated therapy; I didn't trust therapists. I didn't trust anyone. At that point I had just endured a trial in which the people against me were my own family members, even though I had not done anything wrong. A person in the middle of that type of situation learns very quickly to trust no one and feels very stupid and vulnerable for trusting anyone in the first place. With that in mind, how are you supposed to tell your actual problems to a stranger? Today, I am very good at that (after all, here I am spilling my life out on paper for you to read), but at that point in my life, I was not. However, my therapist was creative and got me to do an art therapy project. It didn't involve talking, which was good, because quite frankly I refused to speak in our sessions. The activity involved me building in sand, using figurines, how I saw the world and then describing on paper what I made. With perfect timing, this written document and polaroid picture of the art I did surfaced out of apparently nowhere. I had no idea I still had it in my possession. When I read it, I was blown away to find out that I indeed had considered myself to be in prison decades before I physically went to prison. Here is what that writing piece said (keep in mind I was a teenager when I wrote it):

Today is the 24th of June 1998.

I am writing to record my insight on the world as I have seen it so far in my life.

I am trapped in a prison and there is no way out. I am surrounded by 20-foot walls that keep me in these walls.

I have tried for the past 16 years of my life to escape but have found it to be impossible, but as of today the 24th of June it is going to be possible for me to escape, for I have given myself the power and ability. The people that surround me, laugh at me for they find it humorous that I am locked up. My lover tries to set me free, but it is something only I can do. My foster family tries to understand and help but it feels as though they are not really there. My family is out there somewhere not aware of the pain they are causing me, but yet they seem to think that I am the one to blame for everything wrong that is going on in their lives. There are people being destroyed every day, living lives a lot worse than mine and somehow, I feel as though there is no way to live a life that is worse than mine. There are monsters that keep us all from living the perfect life but somehow and someway some people can live a perfectly happy life in this hole we call the world. There are those that don't care at all of what is in their surroundings and keep doing whatever it is that keeps them happy.

This piece gives you some insight into how my mind-set of the world was forming incorrectly based off my experiences. Feeling like a prisoner and not being accepted your entire life will do some damage inside. When I review many of my writings from throughout my life, including this one, I see that I talk about "starting now, it will be different...." These words come from the self-help techniques I acquired from therapists, self-help books, my own schooling, psychiatric hospitals, etc. The truth is that without a *spiritual* understanding of what is happening, it is impossible to maintain for the long term these "new lives" we keep trying to claim. The devil is not creative. He finds what your weakness is (mine was rejection), and he plays on that weakness in as many ways as he can. His job is to kill, steal and destroy, the Bible says in John 10:10. If he can make you crumble once in a particular way, then he will continue to work on you in that way. The lie I bought into was that I could break free from all the pain I had by dying. He had me convinced in my own thoughts that I would be at peace if I just left this world.

I also have learned that the higher the calling is on your life, the more satan will try to take you out. Now that I am walking in my calling, it makes sense why the devil wanted me dead. People are coming to know Christ Jesus and escape bondage and slavery to sin because I am sharing my story and letting them know that they, too, can have the freedom Jesus brings. It is not a "members only" club. All are welcome to come and be part of the family.

20
In My Strip Cell

After my encounter with God, I figured my circumstances would change miraculously and I could go home. I was wrong. It took me until the second day to get my first free phone call. I only knew my ex-husband's telephone number, so that is who I called. I told him my purse was at the house with my credit cards and asked him to go get it and see about getting me out. He told me not to worry about it; he would see what he could do. I spoke with my daughters on the phone. It was early in the morning, right before they went to school. I played it as cool as possible as I held back from crying. Tears rolled down my face and my throat burned as I told them, "Don't worry. Mommy is okay, and I love you so much." They asked when they would see me, and I could only respond with "as soon as I can." I thought in my head, *I will never see them again.*

My phone call ended, and I cried my way across the annex to my cell. Before, I had always been such a tough person, someone who never cried in front of others. However, at this point, that went out the window. I wasn't trying to be tough anymore. I was as broken as a person could get. I felt it in my bones, in my soul and in my spirit. I had so much shame. It all hit me like a ton of bricks when I didn't have my drugs to numb me anymore.

On suicide watch, the lights never go off. It is a blinding, bright light, especially at 3:00 a.m. when you really start to go through withdrawal. Now, I said my addiction to drugs was gone immediately. What I meant was that the *desire* to use drugs was gone instantaneously. However, the withdrawal process took more than a month. The number of drugs that were in my system on a daily basis was insane. Because I was on such a variety of drugs, the withdrawal was even that much worse. I slept for days. Then I couldn't sleep for days. I was shaky, achy, sweating, having tremors and having seizures; I

WHY I TRIED TO DIE

was irritable and had no energy. I had extreme digestive issues that landed me in medical a few times. They never did anything other than give me Tylenol˚ and Imodium˚. I used to curl up in a ball, in pain, and repeat in my head, "If you never get high again, you will never be sick again." That motivated me. That gave me hope.

There in prison, I was starting to have hope—something that was so foreign to me. I had lived in a state of hopelessness most of my life, and it was exhausting.

Nothing about being in prison is easy. People had told me about prison, but I thought they must be exaggerating. I didn't think that it could possibly be that bad with as much advancements as we have had in our culture. Well, the blinders were now off about that. Prison is as bad as you read about. It is insane. There were rodents and flying cockroaches where I was. Imagine having to take a shower with three other women, and there is a flying cockroach in there with you. You can't use your shoe to kill it because you need your flip flops to keep your feet clean from a filthy floor. Even though we cleaned the shower with the little bit of cleaning product we had, there were breakouts of MRSA and lice on a regular basis. You had to protect yourself. Needless to say, I got over my fear of cockroaches while I hopped around on one foot in the shower chasing a flying cockroach that hissed at me. I was in one of the worst county prisons in Pennsylvania. The smell of the place will never leave my memory.

Nothing, however, compares with how you are treated. I understand it is prison and it is a punishment. It shouldn't be comfortable and a great place to be or people wouldn't care if they went there. The thing is, county prisons are filled with people who are usually not yet convicted. They have not had a trial or been sentenced. Therefore, it is filled with poor, oppressed people. The law says, "innocent until proven guilty," but the system I encountered was quite different from that. I was shocked and appalled. For a long while I thought it was just me, that I was just that cursed that it would happen to me. Only, I discovered this treatment is inflicted *daily* on the poor and oppressed in this country as well as here in Pennsylvania. People think they are making the world safer by locking people up—until it's your family member or loved one who has been thrown in there.

I used my second and last free phone call. After that, unless someone puts money on your phone, you don't call anyone. I called my ex-husband again. Once more he told me not to worry about it; he would do what he could. A few days later nothing had changed, and then I received my first piece of mail. It was from Domestic Relations, saying that my child support was dropped and that my ex had gone for full legal, physical and medical custody. Now I knew I wasn't going anywhere. I cried all day and all night long, thinking about how I would never see my children again.

The chaplain came by my cell and asked if he could do anything for me. (Just recently I became chair of a committee for Restorative Justice and that same chaplain is on that committee with me. There are no coincidences in life.) I asked him to contact my church and ask my pastor to come see me. He offered me a Bible, and I gladly received it. On the cover, it reads, "Free on the Inside Bible." That phrase spoke to my spirit so loud. I randomly opened the Bible and started reading. It was the first time I read the Bible since my encounter with God in my cell. The pages opened to Jeremiah 31:15:

> The LORD says, "A voice is heard in Ramah. It is the sound of weeping and deep sadness. Rachel is weeping for her children. She refuses to be comforted, because they are gone." The LORD says, "Do not weep anymore. Do not let tears fall from your eyes. I will reward you for your work," announces the LORD. "Your children will return from the land of the enemy. So there is hope for your children," announces the LORD. "Your children will return to their own land" (NIrV).

In that moment I decided, now that I was certain God was real, that I knew the Word of God was filled with His truth, I needed to know all it had to say. I had so much to unlearn and so much to learn. Everything I had been taught my whole life was based on lies.

After reading this passage in Jeremiah, I had a choice to make. I could see that God was speaking to me and giving me a promise that I could believe; or I could continue to be devastated and believe my children were gone forever. Later on, I learned what God was really saying in those verses, but in that moment, in where I was, needing to hear from God, He gave me this word and I clung to it. I had my weak moments from time to time; however, I chose faith. I chose to believe in things I could not yet see.

I heard through that Scripture passage God promising to protect my children while I was away from them. I heard Him telling me to focus on me and become everything I am to be, so I can be who they need me to be. So, I did.

Days turned into weeks; weeks turned into months. I tried daily to call my children. I borrowed envelopes or made them and mailed things out to them. Nothing ever came back.

21
J Block

After a week of being in an isolated jail cell, they deemed me safe to go into general population. There were two blocks for the women: J Block was referred to as "the therapeutic block" and K block was known as "the jungle." They called it "the jungle" because some of the women brought the streets into the prison. J block had four dorms on the unit; we didn't have cells. There was a lot more freedom to move around within the unit. However, we had strict rules and a schedule to follow.

As I left solitary to go into general population, I was prepared to fight. I had seen enough movies to know that fighting was something that happened. I had no problems fighting—I was fighting all my life—but something happened when my first fight in prison was about to start. I had a conviction in my spirit not to do it. I had a strong urge that fighting wasn't something I was supposed to do anymore. I thought, *Of all places, Lord, to learn to stop fighting, and You pick prison.* But I was obedient. The almost-fight began with an argument over my refusal to date this girl. I told her that was not what I was there to do, and she was offended. She was talking behind my back and so forth, which was fine, but then she stood behind me in the food line and started talking about how I don't get to see my kids because I'm this and that. She was talking just to start stuff because my children were what I cried for every day. As she said that, I saw red. I always saw red before I fought. Just then they handed me my tray. I thought, *this food or her face*, and just like that I flung my food tray the entire way across the block, getting it everywhere. The correctional officer walked on the block just then; *thank God* she was one of the few chill ones! She turned back around and said, "I'm not doing the paperwork for this," and left. A few of my cellies (cell mates) grabbed me and put me in the cleaning closet—one of only two closets that had doors—and calmed me down. Other cellies of mine cleaned the mess I made. It was nice to have people stick up for me. Before the week was out, the girl who instigated it was moved off the block for her shenanigans.

One of the weirdest things about prison life was that breakfast was served at 3:00 a.m. Lunch was at 10:00 a.m. and dinner at 4:00 p.m. The food was unidentifiable and had absolutely no flavor.

If you asked to go to medical, you would be called out in the middle of the night to go. Medical treatment there is horrible. Sometimes it took three to five days to be seen, and the only medications given out were Tylenol®, Imodium®, and Seroquel®. All pain complaints got the first, all digestive and gut issues got the second, and all mental-health problems got the third.

The showers were open; so were the bathrooms. There was nowhere for any privacy. If you wanted to shave, you had to use a community electric shaver and get someone watch you. You were told when to get up and when to go to bed and when to do everything in between. We were on lockdown sometimes for a week at a time, which meant we couldn't leave our bunk bed unless we were using the bathroom. We had strip searches and room searches in which everything would be tossed. Those searches normally happened in the middle of the night. I hated the sound of the metal door banging when correctional officers (COs) were coming on and off the block.

I was bottom bunk restricted because of a history of seizures. That was a beautiful thing because I actually witnessed people fall off their top bunks and get severely injured. Often when people got injured, they disappeared. At first, I thought they went for medical attention, but I found out afterward they often were put into "the hole" or solitary confinement. I found this out when I started working in laundry as a "blue tag" and delivered all the laundry to the three female areas. I did that every Wednesday. I enjoyed feeling somewhat normal by going to a job. I hadn't been able to work since 2011, and now I was healed enough to work. I then went on to be a "red tag" and worked cleaning in administrative. I felt even more normal at that point, being able to go into the office parts of the building. The walls didn't look like concrete, and I could even talk with staff who weren't guards. They treated me like a human being.

I can't speak for all correctional officers, but I can speak about the majority of the ones with whom I had to interact, and they were brutal. The things they would say and do were the most horrific things I have ever experienced. A great abuse of power happens in prisons. No one has the right to mistreat someone because that person is in prison, no matter what the crime. Correctional officers would instigate fights and abuse power for sexual reasons.

I think it is wrong to have men supervising women, and vice versa. Women were getting pregnant while in prison—and there are no contact visitations.

I personally had a correctional officer who would offer me commissary money for food and hygiene products if I would "come spend time with him." I always declined. He used to call me off the block to set up for religious services and brush up against me inappropriately. I literally threw up in my mouth when he did that, and my skin crawled. He told me that his wife could help me get out because she worked at the courthouse. I declined that offer, too. I refused to sin anymore, even if it meant I had to stay in prison to be free from it. This correctional officer even went so far as to contact me after my release. I told him I would report him if he ever contacted me again.

Another crazy thing that occurred was I didn't get to go outside, ever. Being transported to court was the only time I went outside, and even then, it was for only about the five seconds it took to walk from the front door to the van door. In the van, we sat in the back on metal seats inside cages, like animals.

22

Court Has Been Continued…

My preliminary court hearing was May 30. I figured I would get released that day. I had sat in jail for more than a month and still had not spoken with my attorney once. She was a court-appointed attorney; I could tell she was not thrilled to have my case. When I finally met her, I thought, *Okay, now I can have this all figured out.* I was wrong! Her advice was to waive the preliminary hearing to see what evidence they had. When I went to walk into the room, I passed the person who accused me of these things. She just looked down, not meeting my eyes. I noticed *she* wasn't wearing a tan uniform. I think it is wrong that when someone gets arrested, that person can give up another person for her freedom. Of course, most people will give up someone, whether they tell the truth or lie with a made-up story. I honestly was not mad at her. I knew she was doing what she had to in order to protect herself. I just prayed that she got the help she needed.

The only person who showed up to support me was my landlord. He was there to see if I was okay and to see what he should do with my apartment. He was very kind and compassionate. It meant quite a bit to me that someone who barely knew me showed up, but none of "my people" did. I told the detective and my attorney what actually had happened. I remember them both telling me they believed me. Well, that felt reassuring, but it didn't hold up to be helpful. The detective said the most bizarre thing when I told him I knew who actually was responsible for what I was being accused of. He said, "Okay, let's first get you the help you need, and then worry about that later." News flash, people: prison doesn't bring rehabilitation. It brings institutionaliza-tion and many other things, but rehabilitation is not normally one of them. People who get rehabilitated in prison do so usually as a result of a spiritual reason, not because of the inhumanity they experienced. Most people leave prison with a significant amount of post-traumatic stress disorder (PTSD) that they don't even know they have.

After my preliminary hearing, I went right back to the prison. For the next five months, once a month, I was brought down to the county court-house where I sat in the basement in a cell. At the end of the day, I trudged back out to the van with no one giving me any information about why I wasn't able to make it up to the courtroom. It was so disheartening. We girls on the block would try to console each other when a group came back with long faces on; we knew either they didn't make it to court or did and the news wasn't good.

Finally, on October 6th, I made it upstairs to the courtroom. This was the second time I ever spoke with my attorney. She never came out to the prison to see me. She never returned my requests, letters or calls that were made to her. How does someone represent someone else and do that?! I had written a four-page letter to the judge explaining my side of what had happened. I was really praying he was able to read it. I was handcuffed and shackled when I was brought up from the basement via a special elevator where you have to face the wall, then taken in through the side door of the courtroom and seated where the jury sits.

I scanned the room and saw no one I knew. By this time, I was not sur-prised. I had not received one visitor from the outside while in prison. I had gained a spiritual mentor while in prison; she came to see me once a month, but she couldn't make it to my court hearings, especially because they don't give you any specific time. I think I needed no one to show up for me so I could see that Jesus was all I needed. People will always let us down because humans are imperfect. God, however, will never leave or forsake us. Some-times it requires having everything taken from you to see that God is the one thing that can never be taken from you, no matter how powerful someone is or what circumstances you are in.

My attorney came over to me and told me she had good news for me. My heart was already pounding, and my anxiety was through the roof. The courtroom is an intimidating place when you're the criminal. It is very em-barrassing to think about how people must be looking at you and what they are thinking about you. I tried to imagine no one was in the courtroom. The attorney said, "I can get you out one week from today!" Oh my goodness,

I couldn't believe it! I was finally going to get out! Then she followed up by saying, "But I need you to take a full plea to the charges. If you take this to trial, you will sit here in prison for another year to a year and a half, and it's a 50/50 chance that I can get you out. I don't know what all evidence they have on you. It could go either way. If you are found guilty at trial, you could do five to ten years in prison."

I was never so excited and so upset at the same time. On one hand, I saw myself being able to hug my children while they were young, as opposed to getting out of prison and finding them grown up. On the other hand, the thought of saying I was guilty of something I wasn't made me sick to my stomach. I told her I would have to pray about it. I got in touch with my spiritual advisor and we prayed. We came to the conclusion that it was best to get out and then figure things out from there. There was nothing I could do from inside the prison to prove my innocence.

23

A Whole New Kinda Different

I used my time very wisely in prison. For the first time in my life, I felt like I had something to be sorry for. Most of the time I had suffered at the hands of someone else; not this time. Now I knew God was real, and I was so sorry for all He had witnessed me do to myself. I so regretted how I had cursed His name and blamed Him for all that had happened in my life. The Bible says, "For godly grief produces a repentance not to be regretted and leading to salvation, but worldly grief produces death" (2 Corinthians 7:10 HCSB). Jesus said, "The healthy don't need a doctor, but the sick do. I have not come to call the righteous, but sinners to repentance" (Luke 5:31b-32 HCSB). Romans 2:4 says, "Or do you despise the riches of His kindness, restraint, and patience, not recognizing that God's kindness is intended to lead you to repentance?" (HCSB).

As I read the Word of God with the Holy Spirit living within me, everything on the pages came alive. I learned the heart of God and His forgiveness and love for me. I walked around repeating, "Create a pure and clean heart in me" (see Psalm 51:10). I wanted everything God had for me, and I took this new relationship with Him more seriously than I had anything else. As I read the Scriptures, I prayed for the ability to unlearn the lies I had believed and to apply the truth to my life. As I had checks, or convictions, in my heart, I asked for the ability to change the way I had been. I didn't read the Bible just as something to do; I read it like it was a manual for life, one that worked. I used to read for hours a day. Then I started reading books that were in the library closet that correlated to what the Bible was teaching me. Applying these principles to my life was the most crucial part. I was learning—learning that I had the ability to speak life and death over myself and others; learning that when I forgive, I am forgiven; learning that the tongue is the deadliest weapon; learning that grumbling and complaining is the worship language of satan; learning that all the mind-sets I had accumulated over my lifetime were keeping me in bondage and disconnected from God.

The first mind-set I learned about was the orphan mind-set. The orphan mind-set normally is born out of not being loved or protected properly by your parents. It creates insecurities, jealousy, anger, bitterness, competition and a feeling of not being accepted. Often, when people have the orphan mind-set, they wear masks to cover up how they really feel because they don't want to appear weak. They tend to have raised themselves without proper parenting and so have built a mind-set of not needing anyone or anything to help them. It comes from a place of not having someone when they needed that person. Their exterior is hard as a rock while their inner core is bruised and hurt. When you become a child of God, all of that must go. The Father God loves us because He created us and knew us before we were in our mother's womb. There are no works we can do to earn His love; it just is. He has adopted us into His family, and all our inheritance comes from Him. All that is His, is available to us.

The second mind-set that needs to be dealt with is the victim mind-set. This mind-set normally develops self-pity, and I believe it is one of the trickiest mind-sets because it justifies itself by saying, "But you were a victim." We all have been victimized at some point in our lives; some ways were worse than others. What the victim mind-set does is trap you there in the mind-set you had while you were being victimized. It makes you feel as if people must make up to you for what was done to you, and when they don't, you feel victimized all over again. You expect people to cater to your wounds with unspoken expectations. Subconsciously, you are looking for a savior, normally in a relationship, but when you stay "broken," you blame the person with whom you are in a relationship. The victim mind-set takes the focus off you and projects your responsibility onto someone else.

God calls us to be healed through His Son, Jesus Christ, and His blood. We find our identity in Him, not in man. When my identity was found in what man thought of me, I was worthless and without hope. With all of me, I wanted to please people. I wanted people to see who I was and wanted them to love and approve of me. However, the results were always the same: I felt empty and rejected. I endured so much pain when I didn't have the truth of who God says I am. I believed that I was punished and unloved, but the truth is that I am loved, the beloved of God, and that God is my Father. He never rejects His children. He never forsakes us. He collects ever tear we cry. He knows everything about us, down to how many hairs are on our head. He is the one who saves us, who satisfies the desire for us to be accepted and loved. (Just read Ephesians 1:3-6; Hebrews 13:5; Psalm 56:8; and Matthew 10:30.)

The third mind-set is the poverty mind-set. This mind-set says that there isn't enough. It convinces you that in order for you to have, another person must not have. It promotes scarcity. Often, hoarding comes from this mind-set, as well as criminal activity. Since there isn't enough, you must do what you must in order to get by. That is what happened to me. The Kingdom of God, however, runs on abundance. All things belong to God, and He gives to His children as He desires. He does not want you to look at your needs through worldly eyes. Rather, when you are in alignment with God, He gives to you all the desires of your heart.

So, as you can see, unlearning the old mind-sets and learning these new truths—and many other things the Bible teaches—changed my perspective and my narrative from when I went into prison to when I came out of prison.

24
Bag and Baggage

October 13, 2014, I was brought back down to the courthouse and, just as before, was brought up from the basement in handcuffs and shackles. My attorney sprang some last-minute conditions on me that my getting out would be contingent on, but I already was set on getting out and couldn't imagine sleeping in the prison one more night—even if it meant I would have to register as a "bad guy" for the rest of my life.

I held God's promises in my heart as I went in front of the judge. Maybe it didn't make sense to do that at the time; however, I trusted His Word to be true. Isaiah 54:17 says, "'No weapon formed against you will succeed, and you will refute any accusation raised against you in court. This is the heritage of the LORD's servants, and their righteousness is from Me.' This is the LORD's declaration" (HCSB). I held this verse in my heart. In His perfect timing, I will have my day in court.

As I was called up in front of the judge, I started to weep. As he read my charges one by one, I had to plead guilty out loud. Streams of tears rolled down my face that I couldn't catch because of my cuffs. The tears were not because I was embarrassed or remorseful; I was crying because I was having to lie in order to get out of prison. I was having to say, "Yes, I did something," in a court of law in order to get free from prison. I prayed internally the whole time that God would know my heart and that I would not fear man because I knew God knew that I was not guilty, that I was not what I was being charged with. He protected me through that. The judge finished by saying, "I feel confident in saying I will never see you in this courtroom again." In that moment, I wondered if he had read my letter and knew I was innocent of all this. If he had, how do we have a justice system that allows people to be scared into pleading guilty to something that they aren't guilty of?

How can we have a system that allows for people being charged with things they are innocent of? Is it because they are poor and oppressed and cannot afford representation to fight for them? Is it because these people don't have a support system to stand up and say, "They didn't do that! Why are you doing this to them?"

I take being incarcerated as the biggest eye-opener of my life. As I said earlier, it truly was my "last semester of college." What I experienced was not anything that was discussed in my four years of criminal justice classes or in my two years of applied behavioral analysis classes. This type of treatment is real. It is really happening every day. The poor, the oppressed and those without support systems often get caught up in the justice system because of the environment they were born into. These people are more guilty for who they are than for what they do. If I had come from wealth or had people show up and fight for me, I would not have been forced to plead guilty to something I was innocent of.

Now, in the time leading up to my release, I was trying to work on a home plan. I wanted to go into Christian transitional housing but was denied because of "my kind of charges." There are certain charges deemed worse than others; ones involving fire and anything sexual in nature are in that category. So, I was denied any of that. As a result, I had no idea where I was going when they called, "Bag and baggage."

"Bag and baggage" is what the COs call when you are being released. I was so excited, but so afraid of the unknown at the same time. I went to the front of the jail to get my belongings, which were in a big clear bag. I was considered indigent the whole time I was incarcerated, so the only reason I had soap and shampoo was because other girls gave me their stuff as they left. So, I had no hygiene products with me as I left. My belongings consisted mostly of the pages of my writings while I was inside and, of course, my Bible. They gave me my street clothes—the ones I wore when I was arrested that night. I had put on 50 pounds while inside, not because of the food, which I hardly ate, but because of the Seroquel* they put me on. It makes a person blow up like a balloon. So, I put on my street clothes: my black cami, cheetah-print pajama bottoms, winter boots and coat.

I had missed the whole summer, my favorite months of the year. I had missed my birthday, my niece's birth, and many other things. The hardest day was Mother's Day. Those of us inside set up a spades tournament to keep our minds off the fact that most of us wouldn't be seeing our kids. I had a few black-and-white photos of my kids, and I would rub their faces in the photos and imagine I was touching their soft cheeks.

As I walked out the front door, it was drizzling. The fall air and mist felt like heaven on my skin. I was free! I walked over to the gas station/convenience store. The prison is in the weirdest place: across the street from a toy store and a large mall. In the summer, the inmates could smell the food from the carnival. I used to touch the warm window and daydream about my kids riding the rides, laughing in glee, and eating funnel cake. A tear would roll down my face.

When I got to the gas station, I asked the first guy I saw for a cigarette and a phone. That was a bad habit—asking for a cigarette—but it's what I did. The guy asked what I was in for. People knew when someone had a clear bag that he or she was being released from prison. I minimized my charges, trying to laugh it off, and the next thing this guy does is ask me if I want to go and make some money. I was disgusted, said "no thanks," and walked away. I then asked a woman if I could use her phone, and she allowed me to. I called my spiritual mentor. She said she couldn't come get me but would figure it out. The next thing I know, the clerk from the store told me to come in and get something to eat and drink, that someone had called and paid for it. It was my mentor who did that for me. Soon afterward my brother showed up. He had my purse and my wallet. It was strange to have those things back. When you go without your stuff for so long, then get it back, you discover there is a trauma associated with your things.

My brother took me back to his house and said I could stay with him until I found someplace. Now, anyone who has an older sibling knows that it can be quite difficult living with a brother or sister. I was very thankful, even though it was very humbling living with him. He tended to be a bit bossy since he thought he knew what was right for me. He also had a hard time with me sitting around reading my Bible. He thought it was a waste of my time. He said it was prison thing and would wear off.

One day he asked me, "Have you found the answer yet?" I said, "To what?" He replied, "You are always reading that book. If you didn't find the answer by now, it's probably not in there."

My brother insisted that I find a job and work, but I knew I was not ready. I had my Social Security Disability check to help me pay for rent and gas for the time being. Meanwhile, everything—and I mean *everything*—was overwhelming to me. Within 24 hours I had to report to the state police to get my fingerprints done. The machine had been down when I was released. I also needed to report to probation. I went first to the probation office, and they put an electronic monitoring ankle bracelet on me. I had no notice that

that was happening. I ended up having to wear it for eight months. It was big and clunky and dug into my ankle. It was hard to cover up, but I made sure I got clothes that concealed it.

I was a size I never was before, other than during pregnancy, so not only did I have to find clothes that covered my ankle, but I also had to get clothes that fit. My brother managed a storage unit and, thank God, had units full of things that were left behind. One had a box of clothes just my size. I became very modest in the way I dressed. I still felt dirty from living a life of prostitution and didn't want to appear slutty in any way. I didn't even wear makeup for a long time.

I cried when the probation officer told me all the things I wasn't allowed to do. It felt like I couldn't do anything that was part of a normal life. It was just intimidating. I told her that if I didn't have Jesus, I would go get high because there was no hope in what she had just shared with me.

Then I went to the state police to get my fingerprints done. Again, this was all within 24 hours of being released. When I gave them my driver's license, they quickly came back and told me I was under arrest for a warrant out for me for unpaid parking tickets. I had a panic attack, as I pulled out my bank card to pay for the tickets. They accumulated because my car was parked on the street when I was arrested and every time the street cleaner went by, I got fined. I had no clue that was happening because I was incarcerated the whole time and wasn't getting my mail. The trooper said they didn't want my money and were taking me back down to booking. They handcuffed me to the bench.

I couldn't believe I hadn't even made it out 24 hours and was getting arrested again. They had me lock my purse in my vehicle and brought me down to booking. Booking took me to the district justice where the fines were accumulated, and he said I had already been through enough and released me immediately. He didn't even make me pay the $700 in fines. The police brought me back to booking but wouldn't take me back to my car. Again, I was outside the prison with no money and no phone.

My brother came back to get me; he was not happy about the situation. Once more I was traumatized. By God's grace I didn't get discouraged and kept doing the right thing. I had already had PTSD prior to incarceration, but now I had a serious, complex case of PTSD. I had night terrors and suffered panic attacks almost anytime I was in public. I constantly was afraid of getting arrested at any moment. Loud clanking sounds, people coming up from behind me, not having a quick exit from a room, any sudden movements—all set me up into panic mode.

I had to deal with this fear before I could go to work. I went to the local library and read all the books on Christianity I could find. I had notebooks and wrote things down as I studied. I attended Bible studies and women's groups. I went to a drop-in center for mental health and eventually started volunteering to run groups. I even attended a divorce group because I never dealt with my divorce from a biblical perspective. This group is where I met my spiritual mom. As soon as I saw her, my spirit told me I would be close to her. Sure enough, that happened. I also got a mentor and a therapist and started sharing about my life. I used to ask question after question. I was learning how to live. I was learning how to tell my story. I realized very quickly that if *I* told my story, then no one else could tell my story for me.

25
My Babies

Being away from my babies was by far the hardest thing. That is true for most mothers. It is a unique part about being a woman incarcerated. The other female inmates and I worried every day about how our kids were doing and if they were safe. I remember waking up one night in the middle of the night just knowing that something was going on with one of my children. My heart hurt, and I was anxious. I could feel that one of them was in pain. A mother is bonded to her children this way.

Six months is a long time to have no contact with your children, but it had been even longer since they lived with me. My daughters had been taken by their father in February; hence the nervous breakdown that landed me in the psychiatric hospital at that time. So I had asked my son's father to take him until I got myself together.

Upon my release from prison, my son's dad brought him back to me right away. I was standing on the porch when he arrived, and I ran down the steps and swung open the back door of his dad's car. He was still in a booster seat, only four years old. I just stared at him for a moment, and then he said, "Are you my mommy?" My heart couldn't believe that he could even question that after just six months. But to a young child who doesn't have a comprehension of time, I'm sure it seemed like a lifetime. I said, "Yes, I am your mommy." He touched the side of my face as I got closer, and he said, "You are so beautiful!" I cried as I took him out of his seat and hugged him like I had never hugged that little boy before.

I called my daughters' father. He was not interested in talking with me and was not impressed that I was out. When I asked to see the girls, he responded with, "What makes me know that you aren't just going to go right back in there?" Ouch. That hurt, but I was now a new person. I didn't yell or scream. I didn't threaten or fight. I humbled myself and explained why I wouldn't be going back in. It took a few weeks before he was ready to allow me to see them. My brother and I went and got them from their paternal grandparents' house. They were quiet and shy. I felt, for a little bit, that they were different, that I had lost them. I asked them if they had questions, and they said no. I thought that they would have a hundred questions of why I was gone and what had happened. Instead, they had no clue I was in jail or that I was trying to communicate with them that whole time. There was a strain on our relationship at first. We only got a weekend—Friday evening till Sunday afternoon—together twice a month. It is difficult to rebuild a bond with only four days a month. Slowly but surely, though, they started to trust me again.

They often asked when they could come back and live with me, and I would tell them it was up to God. In a sense, I had to "lay them on the altar" and give up control and my desires for them. Ultimately, learning that my children belong to God and that I had to trust whatever He wanted for them, even if it meant them not being with me, was the hardest lesson I had to learn. Nevertheless, I did things the right way and not the easy way. I didn't want to take shortcuts with our relationship because I wanted something sustainable. I wanted to be a stable, healthy mom. So, I humbled myself before my ex-husband and his girlfriend. I did not grovel or beg. I let who I now was be seen by modeling it. I didn't allow my words to speak for me; rather, I allowed my actions to speak for me. It was the hardest thing I ever had to do. Giving birth to children and then having someone else tell you what to do or not do with them is the most humbling experience one can go through, in my opinion.

It isn't natural to restore relationships this way; however, it is the right way. I remember actually arguing with one of the spiritual counselors in the prison about putting God first and family second. I argued that you have to put your children first or they will not be protected, that it was our job to provide for them. This mind-set is what got me into criminal activity in the first place! I was not willing or even capable during the time of my illegal behaviors of trusting God. It took some time, but I finally understood it.

I now trusted God in all things; I was not doing anything my way now. I kept following God's way as I transitioned from one living situation to the next. Eventually I was living on my own. I used the same thought process with everything now; "slow and steady wins the race." I was willing to go slow and stay low (humble). I wanted to make sure that I was building my foundation properly. I was looking to God for direction, not man, and sometimes that made people wonder if I was even trying to get my life together. Man's way and God's way are quite different, and it can be confusing to people who don't know that difference.

Ultimately, my children came home. The best part is that I never went to court about it. I wanted them to see that their father and I could learn to co-parent. I didn't want to have to have a judge tell us how to be parents. Yes, it was difficult at times, but ultimately it proved to be the best way. I co-parent excellently with both the fathers of my children today, and I think humility and seeking to understand, not be understood, are to thank for that.

> But these things I plan won't happen right away. Slowly, steadily, surely, the time approaches when the vision will be fulfilled. If it seems slow, do not despair, for these things will surely come to pass. Just be patient! They will not be overdue a single day! (Habakkuk 2:3 TLB).

26
Healing Seasons

There was so much to undo. I felt all alone except for Jesus, and honestly, I was okay with that. For so much of my life I aimed to please people and lived through their acceptance or rejection of me. I never really knew who I was or even if I liked me. Most of my life I hated myself because I felt it was my fault that no one loved me or stayed around. I projected how people treated me as the reality of who I was, and all of it was a lie.

As I mentioned in the previous chapter, after I got out of prison, people had a lot of advice for me. I was willing to listen. However, ultimately, I allowed God to lead my steps. I refused to be afraid if people disagreed with me. I just prayed that God would help them see, and I continued to focus on myself.

> Obviously, I'm not trying to win the approval of people, but of God. If pleasing people were my goal, I would not be Christ's servant (Galatians 1:10 NLT).

After living with my brother, I moved in with my new spiritual mother. Unfortunately, she didn't ask her landlord first, and when he found out, he said I wasn't allowed to stay. The lease said only one tenant in the space, or something to that effect. I had two weeks to find somewhere else to go. In those two weeks my spiritual mom was away, so I had the whole apartment to myself. I stayed in prayer and fasting, seeking the Father's way for me. When I heard Him tell me to send an email to the WOW (Women of the Word) group that I was a part of, I was surprised, but obeyed. I was relatively new to the group and still dealt with a lot of pride about asking for help. But, again, I humbled myself and let my needs be known.

Surprisingly enough, someone responded that she thought I was supposed to stay with her and invited me over to her house. It was a beautiful home out in the country; there was this amazing peace there like nothing I could ever have imagined. I could see the sun rise on one side and on the other side I could watch the sun set; both were beautiful every day. God was constantly speaking to me while I was there, sharing with me my purpose and identity. The yard at this lady's house—I can't even put into words how beautiful it was. I compare it to the original garden from Genesis. It was gorgeous. The house had an enclosed porch where I could breathe it all in without the bugs. It was like every flower and bird spoke peace into my life. There is no other way to explain it than that way. I spent my days and evenings reading the Word of God, connecting with Him, receiving healing, and learning who I was. It was one of the most beautiful seasons of my life thus far.

One evening as I sat on the couch drinking tea, reading my Bible, watching the sunset through the trees, God highlighted Isaiah 61 to me. He told me that this passage doesn't just speak of what Jesus was coming to do; He said, "This is your calling." The words of Isaiah 61 jumped and danced off the page and into my heart, soul and spirit. Even today it remains a *knowing* that has never faded but only grows stronger.

> The Spirit of the Lord GOD is on Me, because the LORD has anointed Me to bring good news to the poor. He has sent Me to heal the brokenhearted, to proclaim liberty to the captives and freedom to the prisoners; to proclaim the year of the LORD's favor, and the day of our God's vengeance; to comfort all who mourn, to provide for those who mourn in Zion; to give them a crown of beauty instead of ashes, festive oil instead of mourning, and splendid clothes instead of despair. And they will be called righteous trees, planted by the LORD to glorify Him. They will rebuild the ancient ruins; they will restore the former devastations; they will renew the ruined cities, the devastations of many generations. Strangers will stand and feed your flocks, and foreigners will be your plowmen and vinedressers. But you will be called the LORD's priests; they will speak of you as ministers of our God; you will eat the wealth of the nations, and you will boast in their riches. Because your shame was double, and they cried out, "Disgrace is their portion," therefore, they will possess double in their land, and

eternal joy will be theirs. For I Yahweh love justice; I hate robbery and injustice; I will faithfully reward them and make an everlasting covenant with them. Their descendants will be known among the nations, and their posterity among the peoples. All who see them will recognize that they are a people the LORD has blessed. I greatly rejoice in the LORD, I exult in my God; for He has clothed me with the garments of salvation and wrapped me in a robe of righteousness, as a groom wears a turban and as a bride adorns herself with her jewels. For as the earth produces its growth, and as a garden enables what is sown to spring up, so the Lord GOD will cause righteousness and praise to spring up before all the nations (Isaiah 61 HCSB).

This passage gave me direction. One of the hardest things for me to comprehend was doing work and getting paid. I know this may sound strange, but once I realized all that Jesus had done for me, I wanted to serve Him for the rest of my life without receiving anything for my service. However, we live in a world where everything costs something, and it is impractical to get by this way. The amazing people whom I lived with pushed me to work and move out. However, the idea of living on my own was quite petrifying. I had made a mess of my life the last time I did that, and I honestly was not sure I trusted myself that much yet. I was afraid that if life got tough again, I wouldn't be prepared to deal with it.

The people with whom I was living gave me a deadline to find a place. Rather than live alone, I decided to go live with a new friend whom I had met at the place where I volunteered. I didn't know it prior to moving in, but her son was into illegal activity. The location also was awful. A bar was next door; fights often broke out in the middle of the street. Sometimes gunshots echoed down the street. I hated feeling the oppression that was so familiar to me. Before, I didn't understand what oppression was. Growing up in it made me think it was just normal. Once you are free from it, though, you can tangibly feel it in the air.

Living here put me at risk. Being on probation, I was not to be around illegal activity. It very easily could have jammed up my life again. I felt the Lord pulling me toward service at a local diner. I'm going to be 100 percent honest and say I was insulted when I heard Him say that was where He wanted me to work. After all, I was educated and equipped to do so much more than that. Finally, after things were getting tight and I had to move out of the amazing, peaceful house I was at, I walked into the diner. Instantly, I understood why

I was being called to work there. Not everyone will go to a church. Neither will everyone go to a therapist. But everyone, and I mean *everyone*, eats! It made perfect sense.

Working there, I became even more bold in the spiritual gifts the Lord had given to me and started to speak life into people as they ordered food. God would give me words of knowledge, and I would just pour love into every customer I had. Sometimes I was bold enough to openly ask if I could pray or give a word that I was hearing from God. It was amazing—especially because my bosses were Egyptian and Muslim! I never was told to stop.

I saved my money and eventually was ready to get my first apartment. Having felonies really prevents you from getting apartments. However, once again I found favor with a church member who had an apartment above her business, and I rented that. She blessed me with a rental fee that really only paid the utilities. My faith in people was starting to grow and become strengthened.

I felt the leading to go to a different restaurant, and when I got there, I knew it was where I was supposed to be. I worked there for three years, putting in the effort as if it were my own business. I no longer was ashamed that I was "only a server"; I realized that I was a servant of God, and I enjoyed my job very much. I got to share the gospel with co-workers and customers. I used to imagine I simply had a really big kitchen and had invited people over to eat. It was such a pleasure and honor to be able to serve God through serving people. My bosses, on the other hand, were a little more difficult. They were not huge fans of complimenting or giving respect to people, especially women. Some of that was their culture, I believe. Still, I prayed and continued to be myself. I learned how to use brave communication and conflict-resolution techniques.

It was in this season that my children returned home to me. Everything was starting to unfold perfectly. I started to understand that sometimes God must make us uncomfortable or we won't move, either because of fear or complacency.

Once again, I had to move. This time I had to relocate because the business owner was doing demolition to redo the business. I was happy for my landlord but also devastated for a moment for myself. Then the thought came that maybe it was time for me to buy a house. I found a beautiful home that was perfect for what I needed and wanted. The inspection found there were some big-ticket items needing repair that made it not worth the price. However, the owner also owned the house next door and was renting it out. So, the children and I moved in there. He eventually sold that house, but the original house I wanted never sold. Today I am living in that house. God is good.

27
Trust Who?

As you can imagine, I had grown up learning that no one was safe. Now that my life was back on track after prison, I became quite content with spending all my time with Jesus and my children. I attended any and all services while in prison; when I got out, I went to church on Sunday but spoke very little with other people except for small talk. I had not quite found my voice yet. I also struggled with fearing that people would not accept me if and when they found out that I had been in prison. I was like a sponge regarding my relationship with God, soaking up everything I could about Jesus and God and Holy Spirit, but I didn't want friends.

Slowly, as I watched people, I found one or two safe people and would share with them. I was always praying for boldness. I knew that in order to do what God had called me to do, I couldn't be afraid. However, people can be so judgmental. I had to stiffen my backbone a little more, so I started sharing in small groups. I still was cautious of what information I shared because, as I listened to people speak, I could see that, even as Christians, there were things that weren't acceptable to them. I continued to pray for mercy for them and for open doors for me to be bolder.

I grieved while in prison that I would never work with children again because of my felonies and what I was charged with. I remember crying out to God with groans of regret for not understanding when He spoke to me as a child and told me I would be a safe haven for His children. He told me, "That word is still the same for you; the perspective is just different. I said you will be a safe haven for My children. All people whom I call and who receive Me are 'My children.'" What an exciting moment that was when I realized that it *was* God who had spoken to me all those years before, when I was only six years old. It wasn't just my imagination.

I started mentoring people as I volunteered and worked at my job. Anyone who wanted to know about Jesus or how I was able to change my life around, I was willing to share my story with. I learned how important my story was, and I got a little bit bolder.

Then, a little more than a year ago at this writing, God had to make me uncomfortable. I had gotten too complacent serving food. He wanted me to move into my next season, and I was afraid to face the rejection I was certain would be on my way there. Because I wasn't even willing to try, I believe the Lord moved my hand for me. I didn't get fired or quit, but the restaurant hired a new manager, and we didn't see eye to eye. Within a week of her taking the position, I was off the schedule. I went four months without work. It was a testing of my faith. Did I indeed believe to the level I said I did? On top of that, my financial accounts were cyber hacked. Still, I trusted in Him during that trying time in 2018. It was difficult, but it was necessary. God always showed up, even if it was at the last second.

The Lord had built my trust in Him through His provision and an abundance of blessings. In 2015, the government gave me $24,000 because they said my children should have been receiving benefits while I was receiving SSDI. The government doesn't do that! That was my Father. Other miraculous funding came basically out of the sky. For instance, I went to the doctor and the doctor's office later gave me a check, saying they overcharged me. Again, this doesn't happen. I was able to take my credit score from 540 to 760 in two years and get out of a $90,000 debt, which included all my student loans being paid. It's easy to trust God when He's blessing you, but it is a little more challenging to trust Him when trials come your way and it looks like you might not make it.

During this time that I wasn't working, I started praying that I could have a job doing all the things I do for God, just loving people, helping them get set free, and being a voice for the voiceless. During a volunteer meeting at Friends Over Fences (a local program that helps ex-offenders), the leader suggested I reach out to a reentry program that was providing mentoring. Before I knew it, I was part of the family. Now I get to do so many amazing things that go beyond what I could ever have imagined. I share my story at churches; at universities; at law enforcement conferences, trainings and meetings; and even with county and state authorities. I mentor and facilitate groups. I get to walk in the front door of the prison I used to be in and attend meetings there. My input is important and valuable as a reentrant. I also became a certified recovery specialist with the state of Pennsylvania. I have the honor and privilege of meeting people in the ER when they are under the influence of drugs or alcohol and are interested in getting help. I get them connected with services. The best part about all my work, though, is I get to share what Jesus has done for me. I love all the things I do. I serve the Lord every day of my life.

I am still on a journey. One big thing I continue to struggle with—it has been my focus this past year—is trusting people. Trusting God has become very easy for me; trusting people, not so much. God has given me an amazing church family that I call my tribe, the family I chose. I also have an amazing fiancée whom I will have married by the time this book is published. He is loving and kind and doesn't judge any of my past. My family has come back into my life, and most of my siblings and I have reunited. (Unfortunately, I lost one of my younger brothers, Ian Christopher, to suicide in the summer of 2017.) As for my parents, I have been able to forgive both of them after I realized that I had expectations of them that they could never fulfill. They couldn't give me what they didn't have, and even now they aren't who I wanted them to be as parents. Nevertheless, I still love them, forgive them and honor them. My father has come to know Jesus, which is such a big answer to prayer. He will be walking me down the aisle at my wedding. I never even dreamed that was something that could happen. That is the power of forgiveness.

God has placed amazing people in my life today who accept me and love me as I am. That is such a blessing to me. Often, I still feel handicapped in relationships because there is always this lurking fear that people are still not safe. I have to fight this fear with all my might, and I do. As I walk this path, I am confident that I will continue to strengthen this area and be able to have long-lasting friendships. I got a new lease on life back in 2014, and I don't take it for granted—not one bit. Every day is an amazing day to be alive. I used to daydream of dying, and now I wake up grateful for being *so alive*!

28
My Voice

I would be lying if I told you that my life is perfect now and every day is a picnic. There is no such thing as a perfect life. What I can tell you is that through hard work and consistency in doing the right thing, life got easier. The world doesn't feel like it's falling apart every other day. Believe it or not, a person who is used to continuous crisis and chaos will actually go through withdrawal when it stops. Things in my life still go wrong; however, I am now equipped to deal with those issues in a healthy manner. I'm not just talking about coping skills. Though such skills are beneficial, they alone cannot sustain you. There is a point at which you understand your purpose and identity; thus, it would only make sense for the enemy, satan, to want to discourage, distract and even divert your attention to anything other than what you are called to do. Sometimes he makes the distractions really beautiful and "sparkly," making it hard to discern that those things are meant to take your eyes off what you're supposed to be focused on. As you learn and grow and mature as a new person, you become aware of these things.

Whenever I feel weak, God reminds me to depend on Him, to rest in Him. He helps me keep my eyes focused on Him. If everything was perfect, we likely would think we no longer needed a close relationship with our Father God. Paul the apostle said, in effect, that he was quite happy with the thorn: "That's why I take pleasure in my weaknesses....For when I am weak, then I am strong" (2 Corinthians 12:10 NLT). The less I have, the more I depend on Him.

I took out all idols I used in the past to comfort me—even the legal things, such as cigarettes, eating and sex. So many times, we replace one addiction with another and justify the switch because it's legal. The truth is, anything you use to try to avoid pain, emotion or reality is an addiction. You must get to a point where you feel your feelings and are okay with it—even the not-so-pretty feelings. Why? Then you can deal with the issue. Dealing with the shame, anger and pain of what was done to you and what you have done to yourself is hard, but it is worth it once you forgive and let go. Then those emotions aren't lying dormant in your soul, waiting to emerge again when they have a chance. As a result, you become free. You can be transparent and vulnerable and not feel yucky while you do so. That is how I got to the place where I can speak before large groups of strangers and not be embarrassed. *I own my story.* It is my story, and no one else can speak it for me. They can't say what is right and wrong or anything, really, because it is mine. Once I got to this place, I discovered it was a game changer.

I never felt heard as a child. I never felt that my voice was important. When I did try to speak at different points in my life, people didn't listen. People didn't believe me. They didn't help me when I asked for help. I was always made to look like the bad guy. I assure you, that can take you to a place where you don't *ever* want to speak.

I wore a mask for most of my life. I used humor and sarcasm to cover up how I really felt. Being vulnerable as a child left me wounded and hurt. I never felt safe in any environment. I felt dirty and gross. I believed it was better to blend in and just try to get people to like me. I turned into a chameleon. I adapted and blended into my surroundings and became like the people I was around. This adaptability is an amazing skill, but because I grew up without an identity, it got me caught up in a lot of things that caused me even more pain. I didn't grow up with strong morals and values, and because I lived in so many different homes with so many different people, nothing was ever consistent.

I have done a lot of things I didn't want to do because I didn't think I had the right to say I didn't want to do them. Other times I just wanted to be liked, to be cool, or whatever you want to call it. Today I try my hardest to teach my kids how stupid this thinking is. I try to teach them identity and purpose and uniqueness so they don't get caught up in this nonsense.

Now that I have my voice, people know I have something to say. I am quick to listen and slow to speak; however, when something needs to be said, I say it. I don't let people walk on me and use me anymore. I have healthy boundaries, and I make sure my yes means yes and my no means no. I never want to forget how I used to feel because there are so many people who still feel this way. I share my story as much as possible to help those who are stuck in those mind-sets to know they can get out. As for the people who work with these individuals or who simply don't understand, I pray that my story helps them understand better. So many people in the world are suffering in silence and oppression. They just need people to ask if they can help, even if it's just by listening and encouraging them. We don't have to have all the answers or solutions. Rather, the most important thing we can do for people is to let them know that they are seen and that they are loved. No matter how different people are from one another, there are some things that stay the same: we are all human beings; we all need connection, acceptance and love; and we all need hope.

I am thankful for the pure heart God gave to me at a young age. The heart reveals your true self. Although my heart, at one point, was cold, hard and bitter, it was formed that way to protect myself from this world. I once had a heart that looked like a thousand bullets had shot holes through it. One by one, Jesus healed those wounds with His love. It is the only thing that truly heals us.

In one sense, my journey has just begun. So, until we meet again, take care of yourself. You only have one life.

Invitation to Freedom

I am just so blown away by what God has done for me! One thing I know for sure about Father God—my Abba, my Daddy—is that He is not a respecter of persons. That basically means that what He has done for one person, He will do for another. So, if you have been intrigued by reading my story and learning how I came to know God through the hardest times of my life, I want to invite you to join me in this freedom. You can have the same freedom I have today—freedom from any bondage or sin you are living in and want to escape from. There is no specific prayer or formula to gain this freedom, but I can guide you with a simple prayer and you can add to it whatever is on your heart:

> Father God,
> Thank You for allowing Your Son, Jesus, to die for me so that I may have eternal life and have a relationship with You. I surrender my life to You. I repent for my sin and ask for forgiveness. I don't want to do things my way anymore. I want to live a life that is obedient to You and to Your will for my life. I ask that You give me a clean and pure heart. Show me how to live like Jesus did. Fill me with the Holy Spirit, so that Your Spirit lives and works within me.
>
> Break my heart for what breaks Yours. Let me see like You see, talk like You talk, hear like You hear. Let my hands be Your hands and my feet, Your feet.
>
> Fill me with Your love, peace, hope and joy. Help me to see and discern my identity and purpose. I ask that all shame be

removed from me today and that today be the first day of my new life. Make me brand-new.

I ask all these things in the mighty, powerful and beautiful name of Jesus Christ, my Lord and Savior! Amen.

CPSIA information can be obtained
at www.ICGtesting.com
Printed in the USA
LVHW050138151221
706185LV00022B/2829